N.O.K.

# NEXT OF KIN

Inbal Abergil

Daylight

Cofounders: Taj Forer and Michael Itkoff
Creative director: Ursula Damm
Copy editor: Elissa Rabellino



ISBN 978-1-942084-35-8

Printed by Artron, China



Daylight Books
Email: info@daylightbooks.org
Web: www.daylightbooks.org

*For my mother, Fabian*

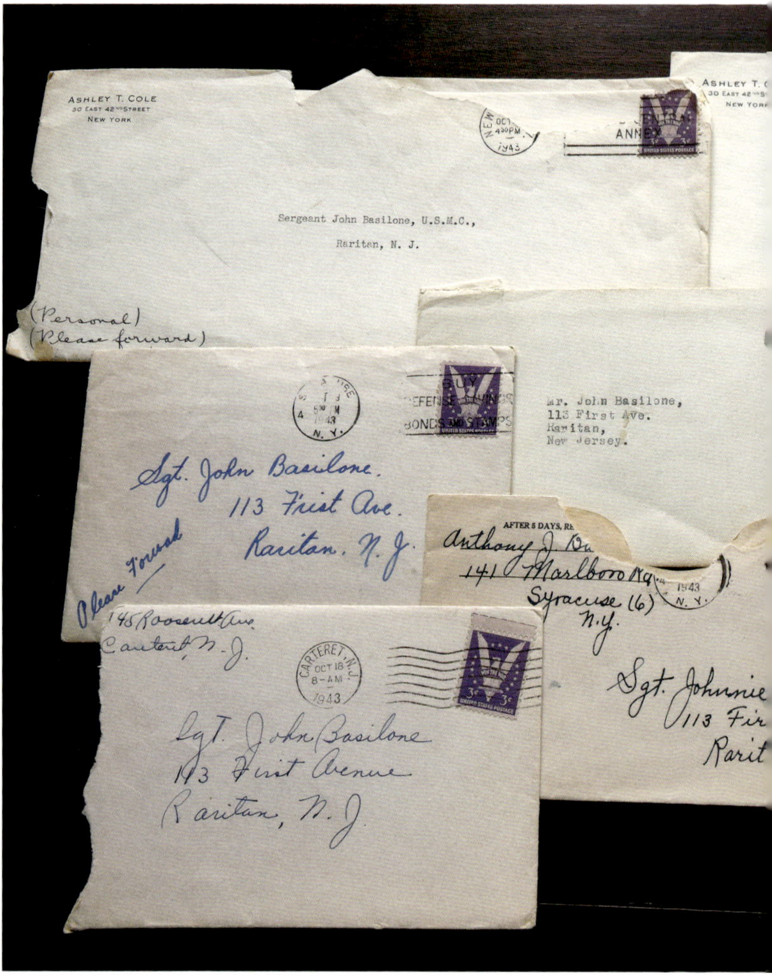

Ashley T. Cole
30 East 42nd Street
New York
Sergeant John Basilone, U.S.M.C.,
Raritan, N. J.
(Personal)
(Please forward)
Mr. John Basilone,
113 First Ave.
Raritan,
New Jersey.
Sgt. John Basilone.
113 First Ave.
Raritan. N. J.
Please Forward
Carteret, N.J.
Sgt. John Basilone
113 First Avenue
Raritan, N. J.
Syracuse (6)
N.Y.

# BASILONE

NEW YORK, N.Y.
SEP 22
3:30 PM
1943
GRAND CENTRAL
ANNEX
John Basilone, U.S.M.C.,
onal Medal of Honor,
Raritan, N. J.
BOUND BROOK, N.J.
SEP 9
6:30 PM
1943
Mr. John Basilone
113 First Ave.,
Raritan, New Jersey.
PHILADELPHIA, PA. 9
OCT 3
6-PM
1943
BUY
WAR SAV
BONDS AND ST
Platoon Sargeant John Basilone
United States Marine Corps.
Raritan.
New Jersey.
St Annes Parish Rectory

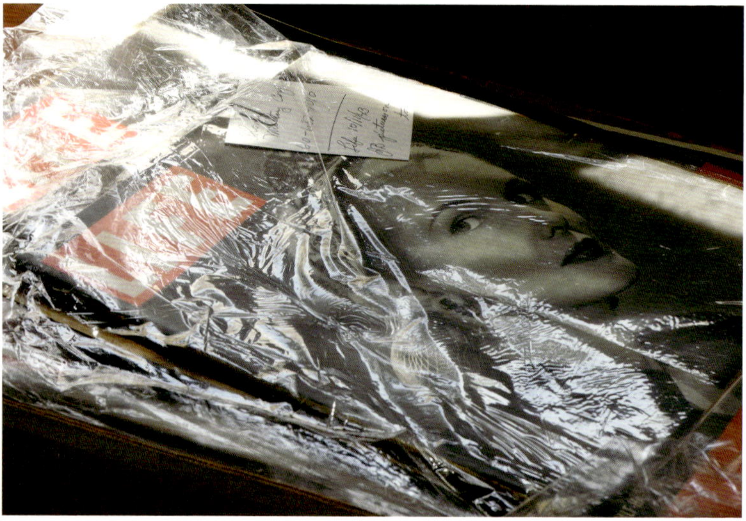

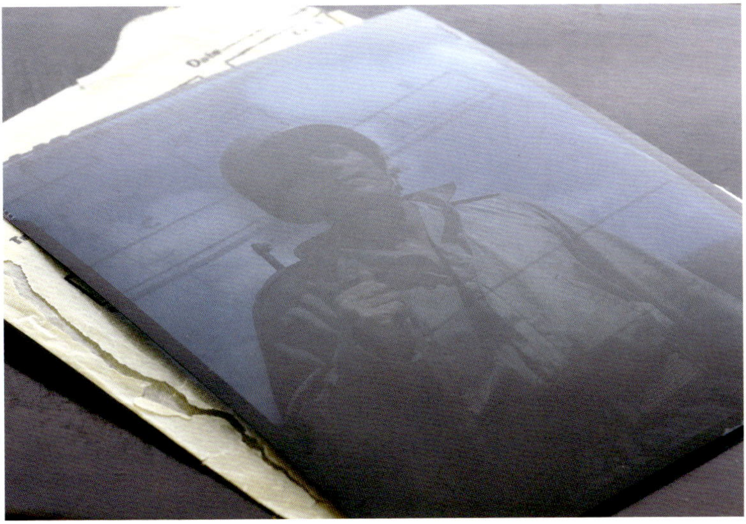
Date

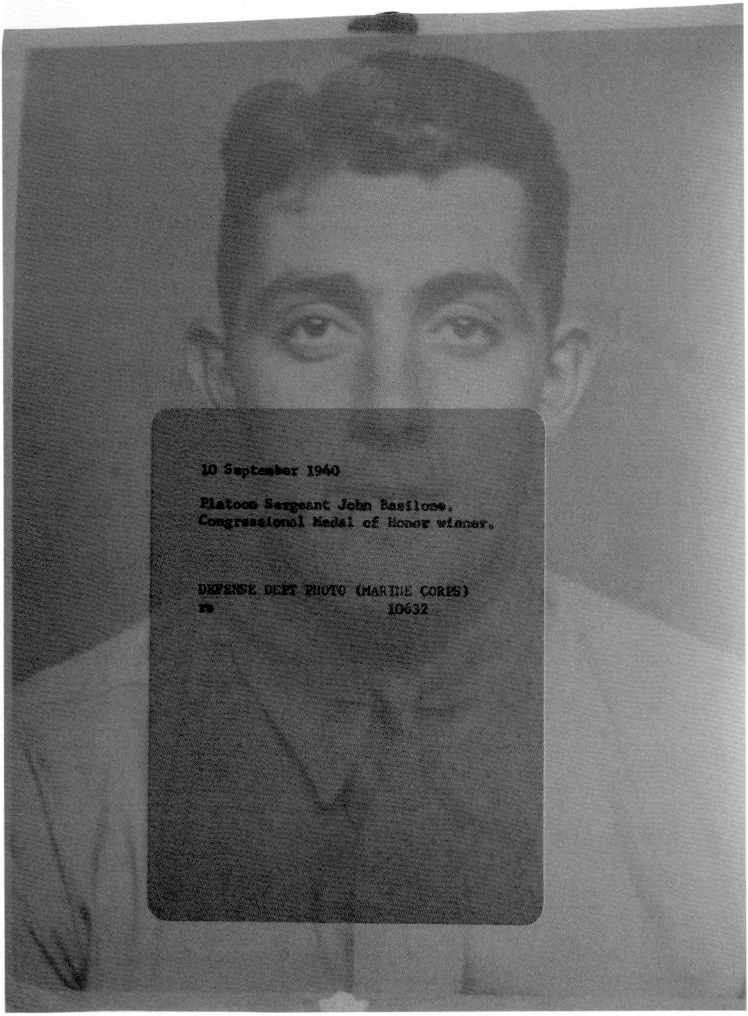
10 September 1940
Platoon Sergeant John Basilone.
Congressional Medal of Honor winner.
DEFENSE DEPT PHOTO (MARINE CORPS)
10632

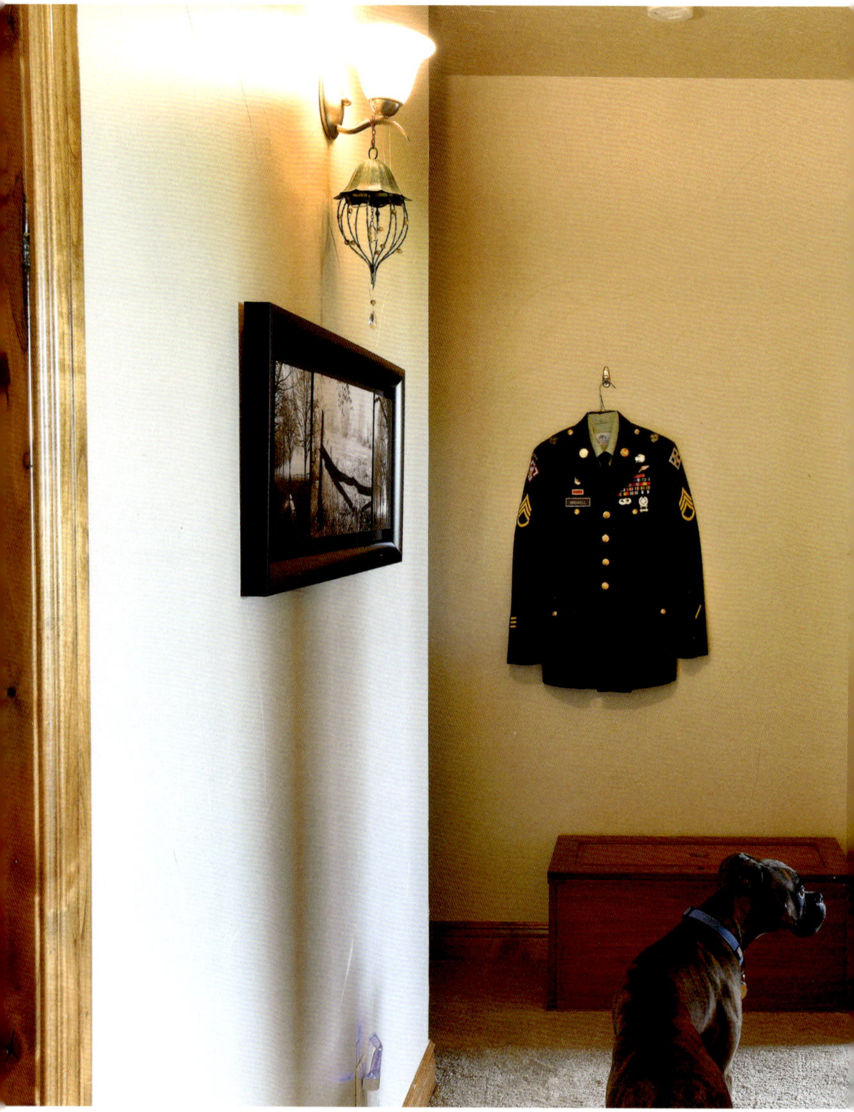

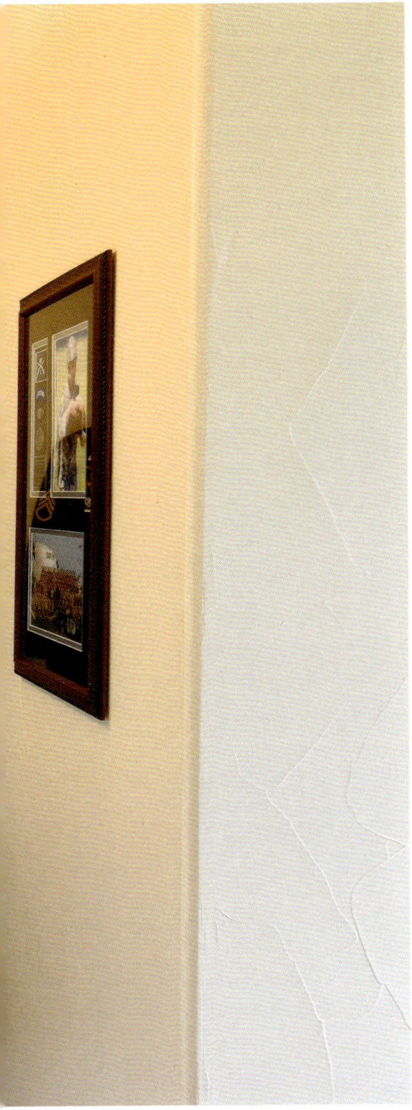

# BIRDWELL

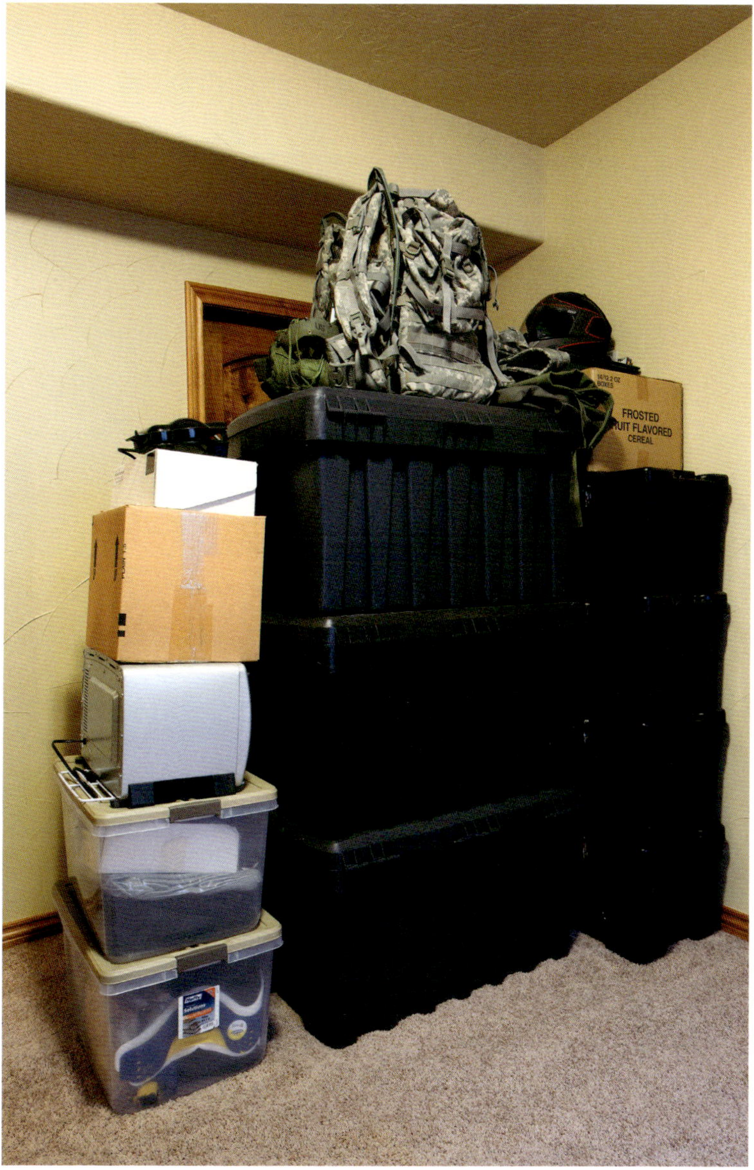
14/12.2 OZ
BOXES
FROSTED
CEREAL

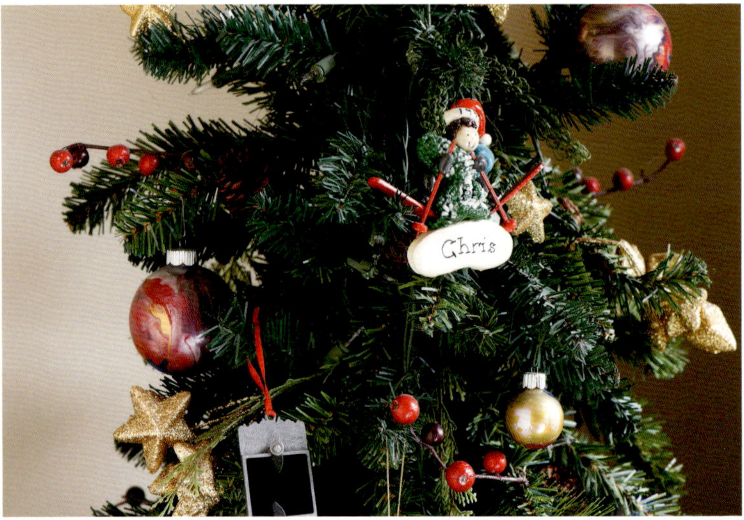
Chris

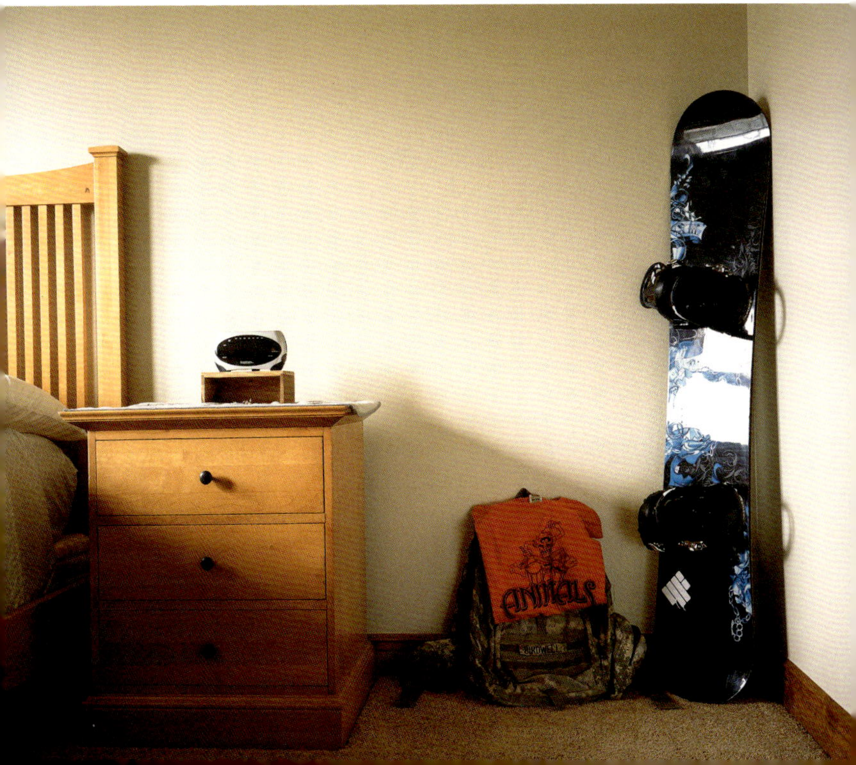
ANIMALS

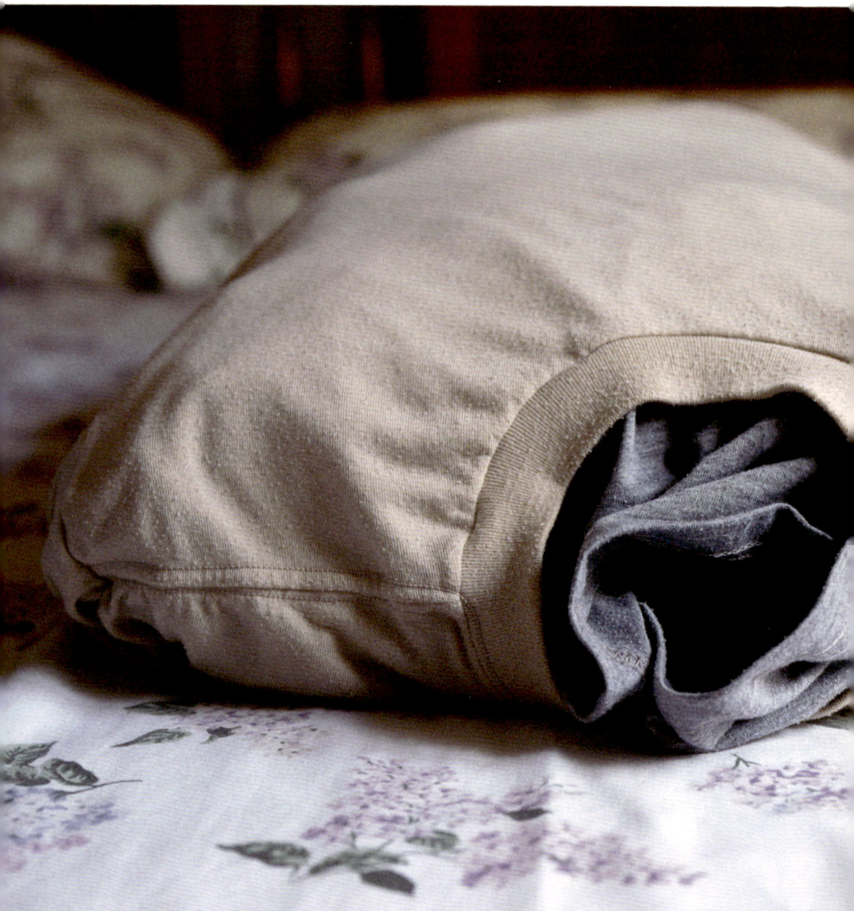

# CORTES

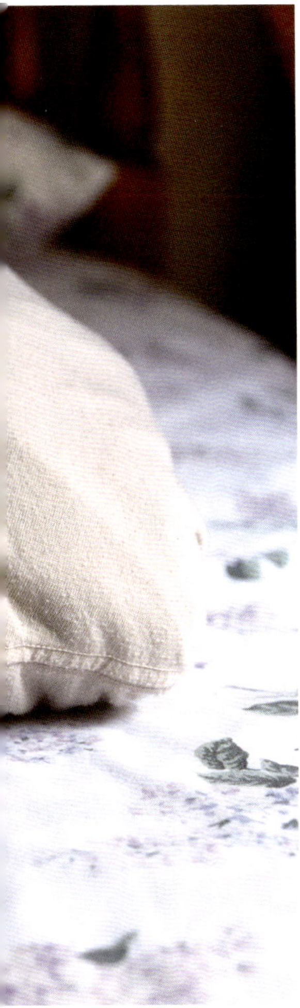

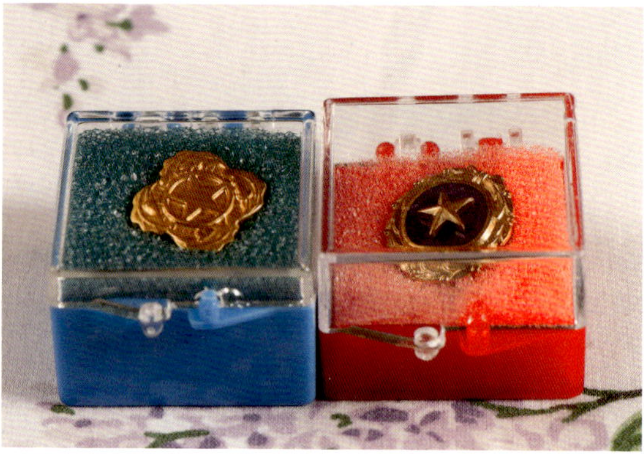

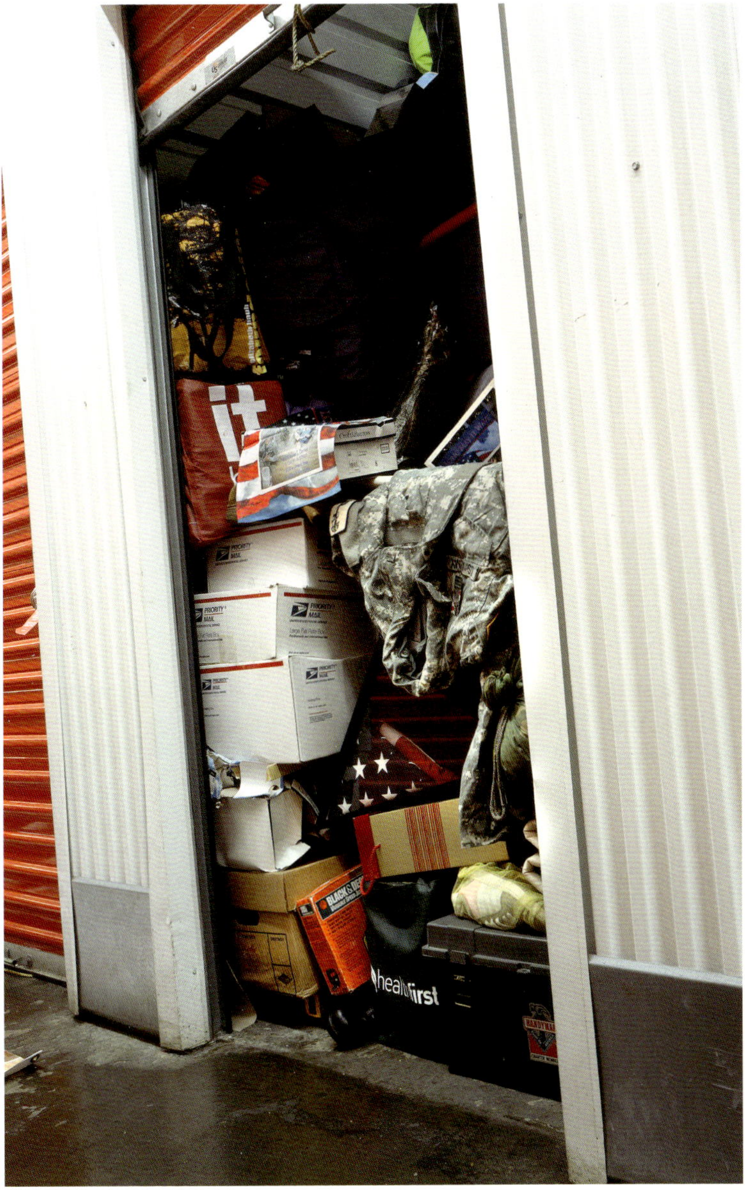
healthfirst

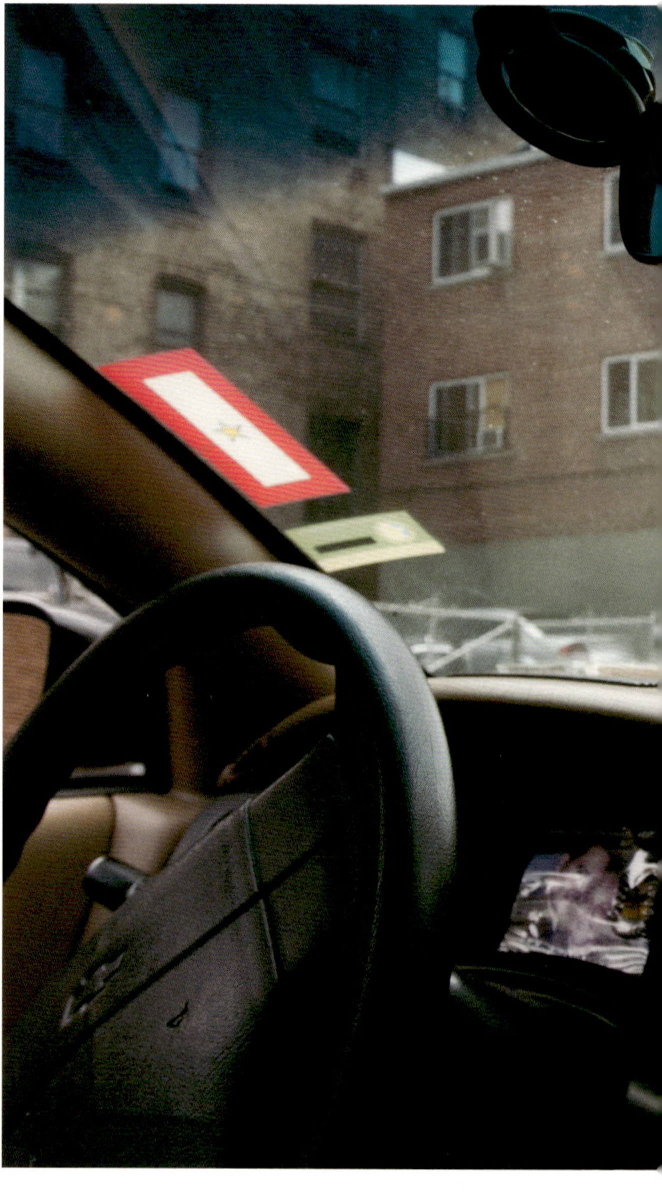

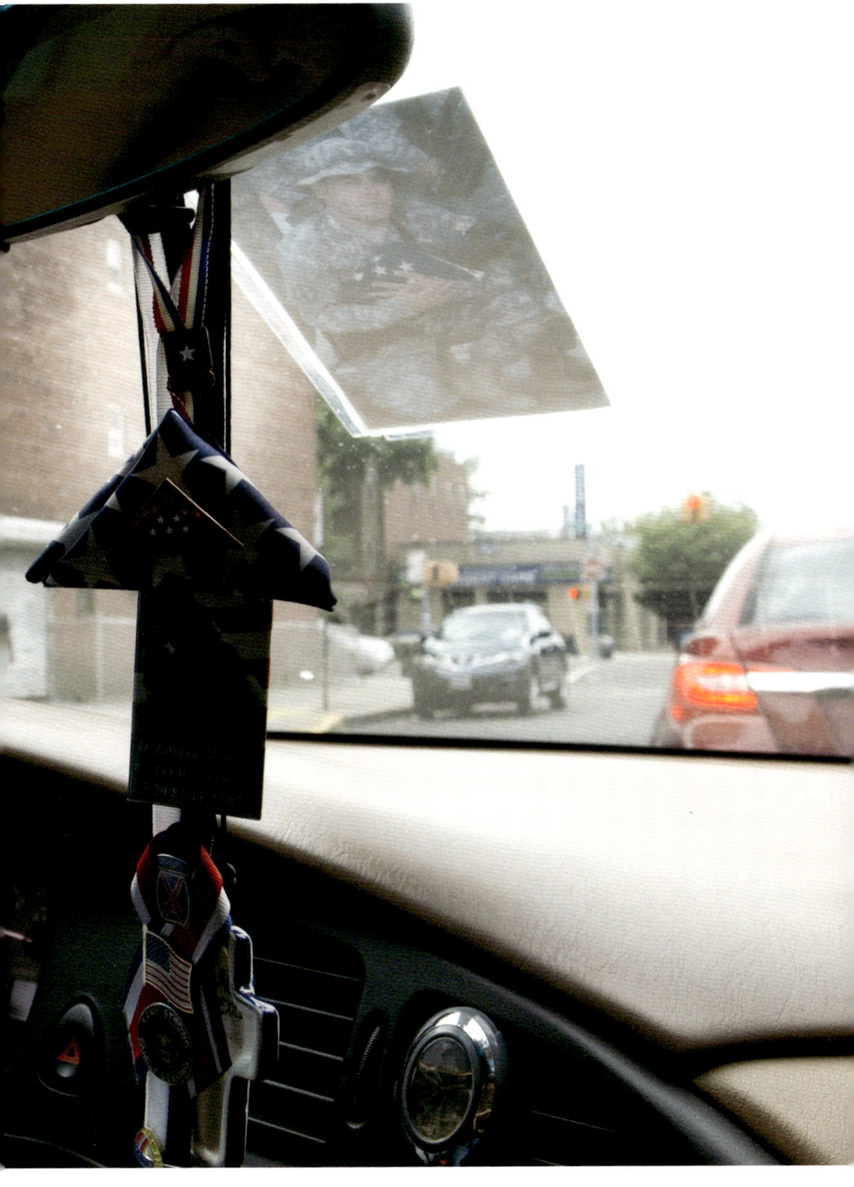

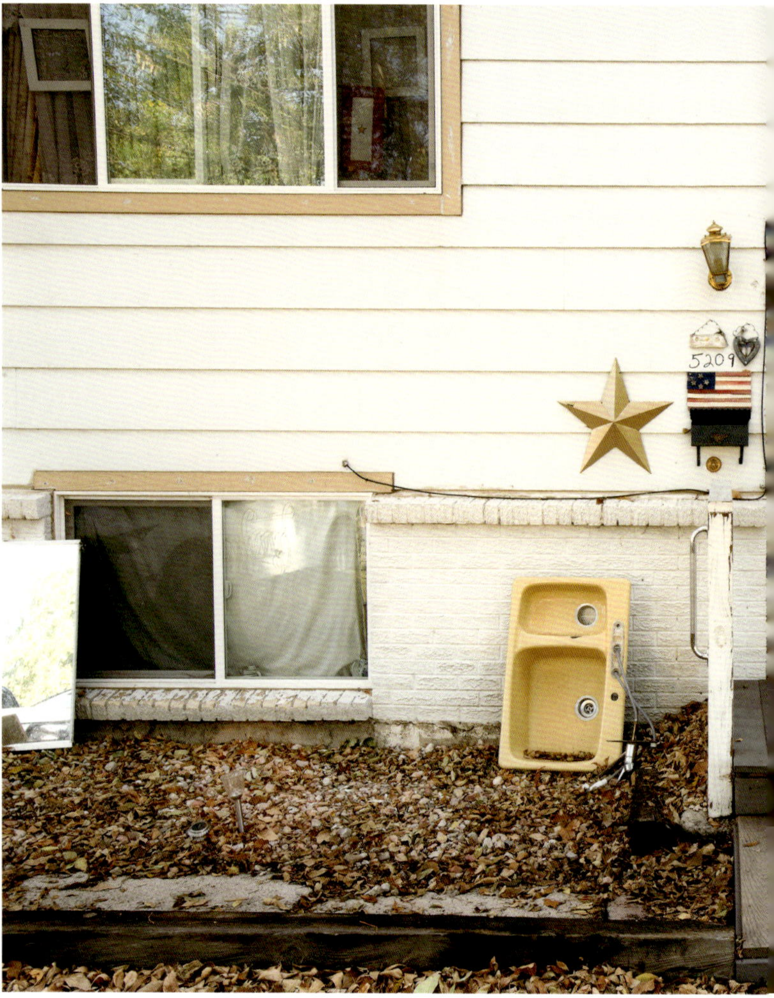
5209

# DOMELJ

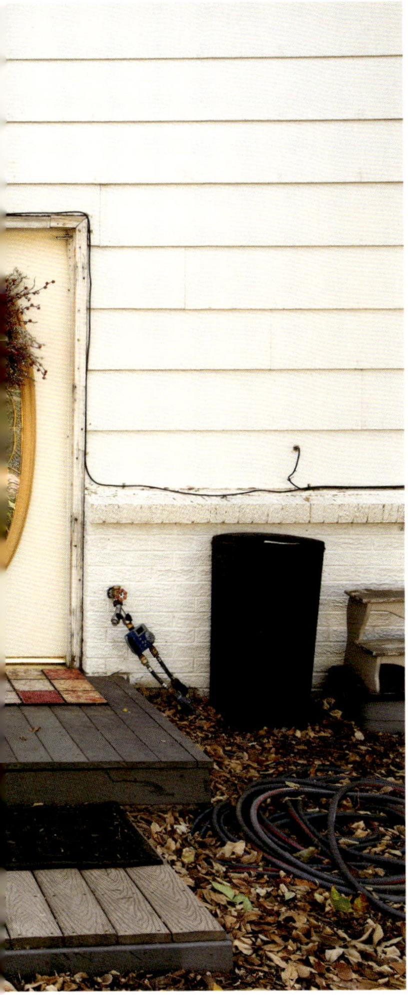

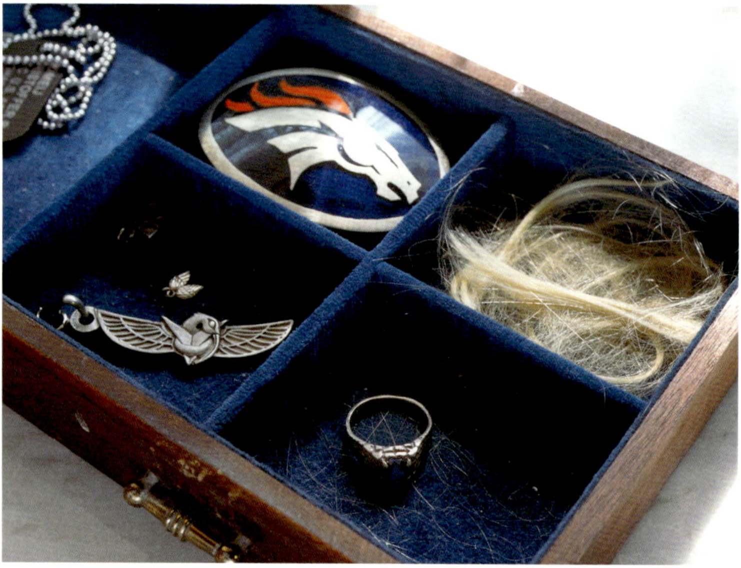

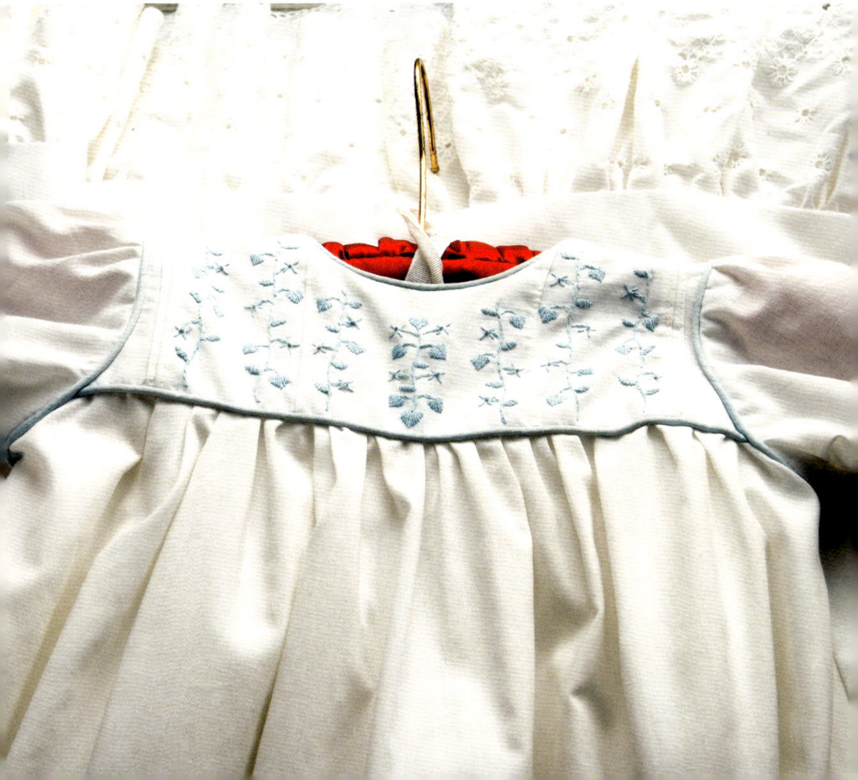

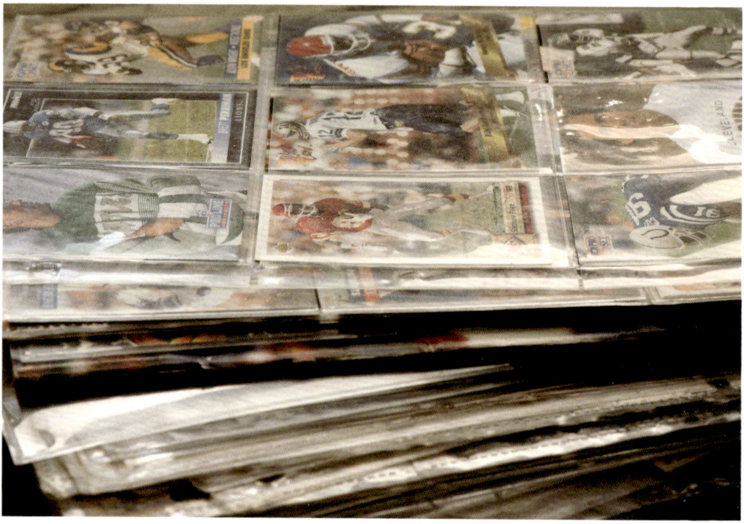

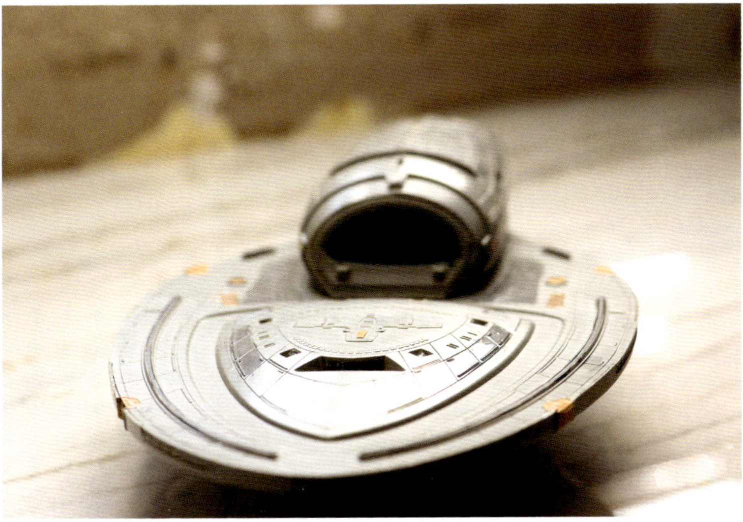

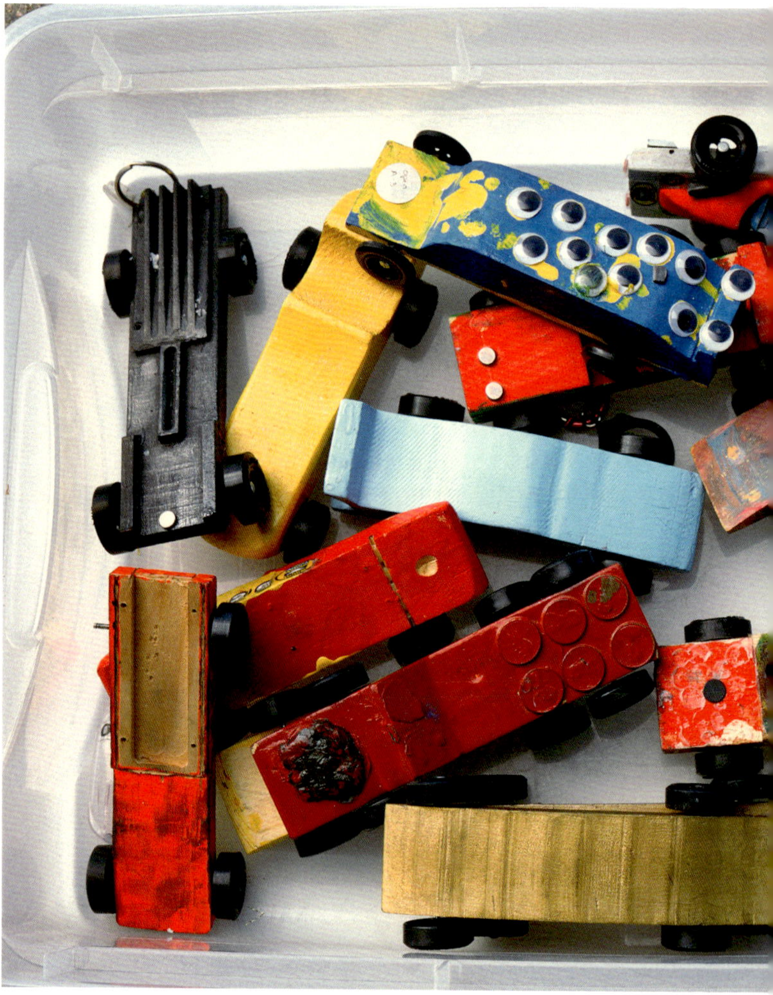

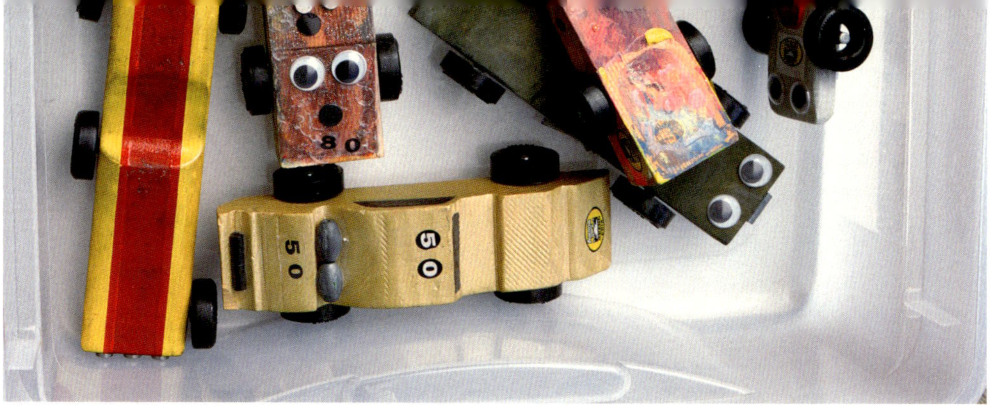


# GOETZ

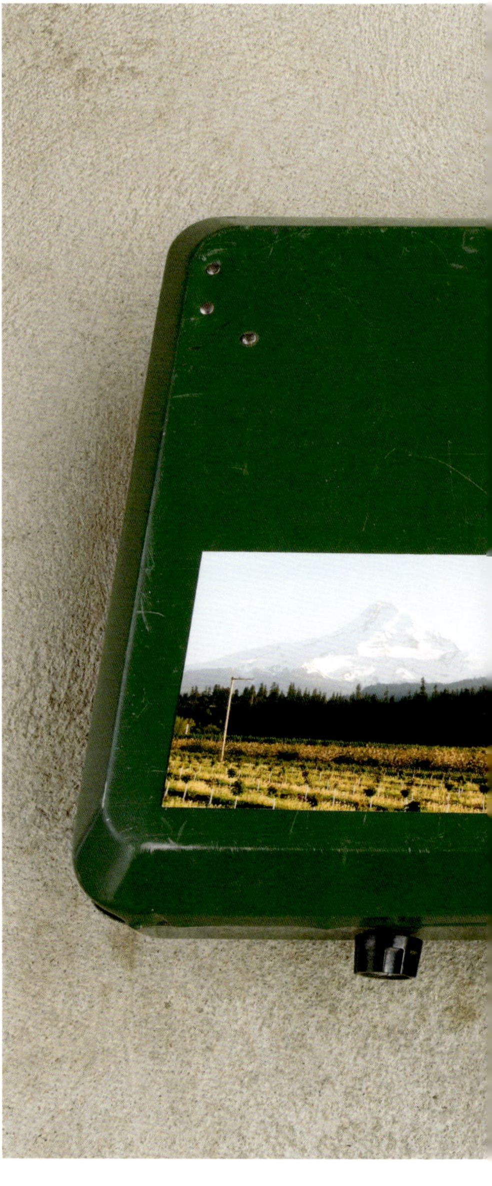

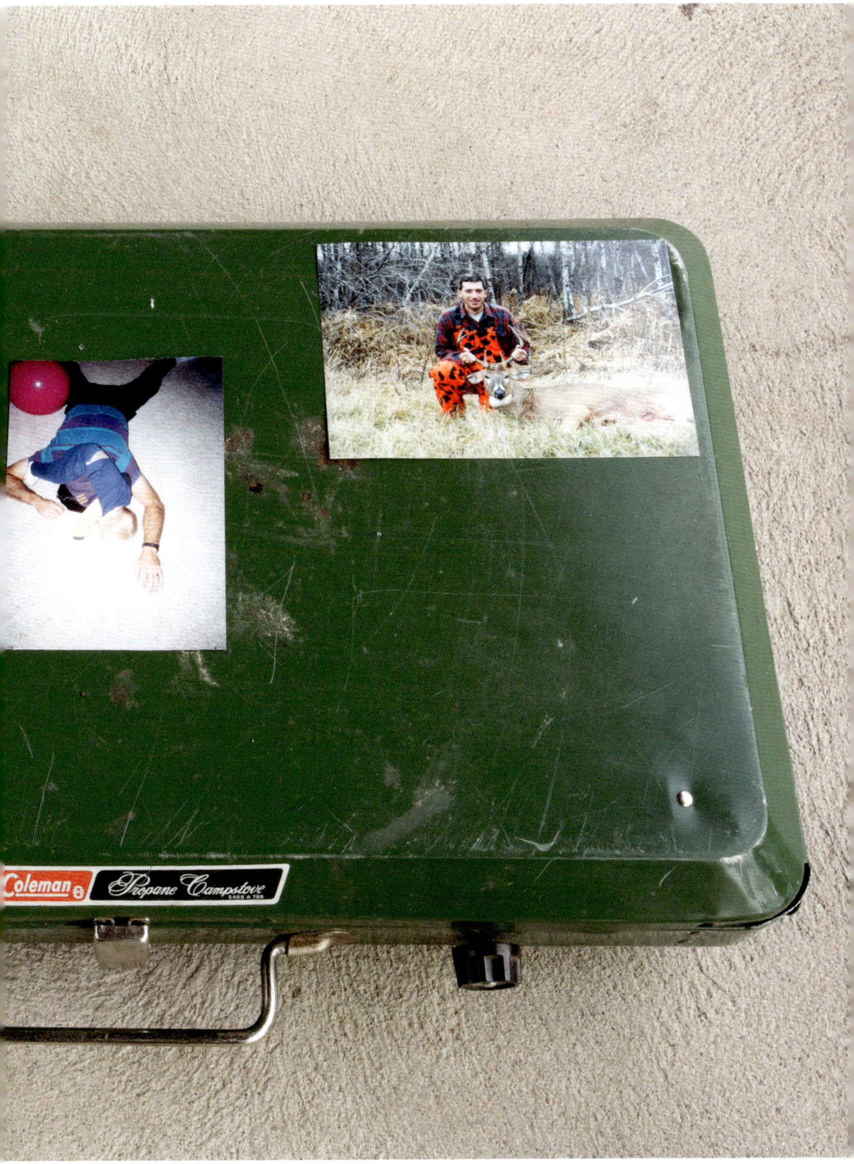
Coleman
Propane Campstove
5400 A 700

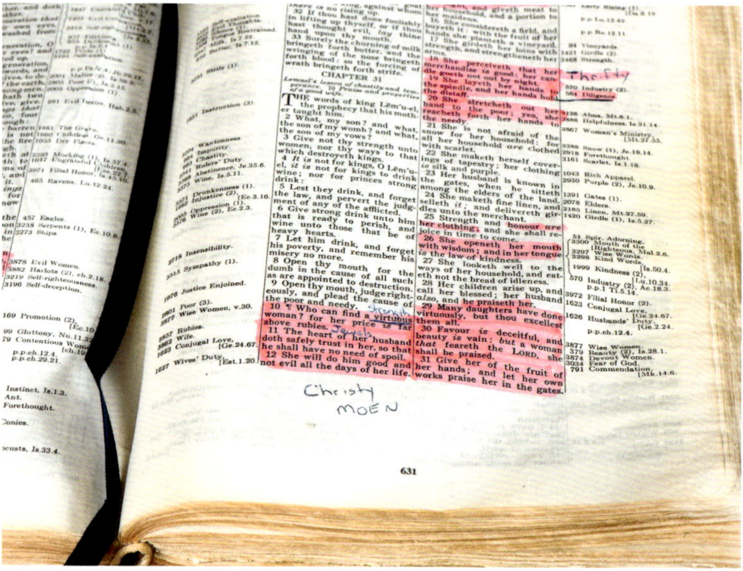
CHAPTER 31
Thrifty
Strength
Jewels
Christy
MOEN
631

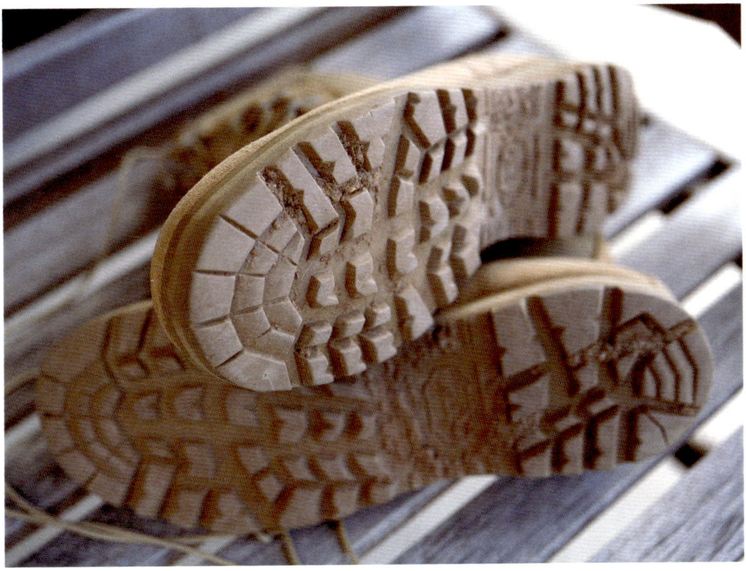

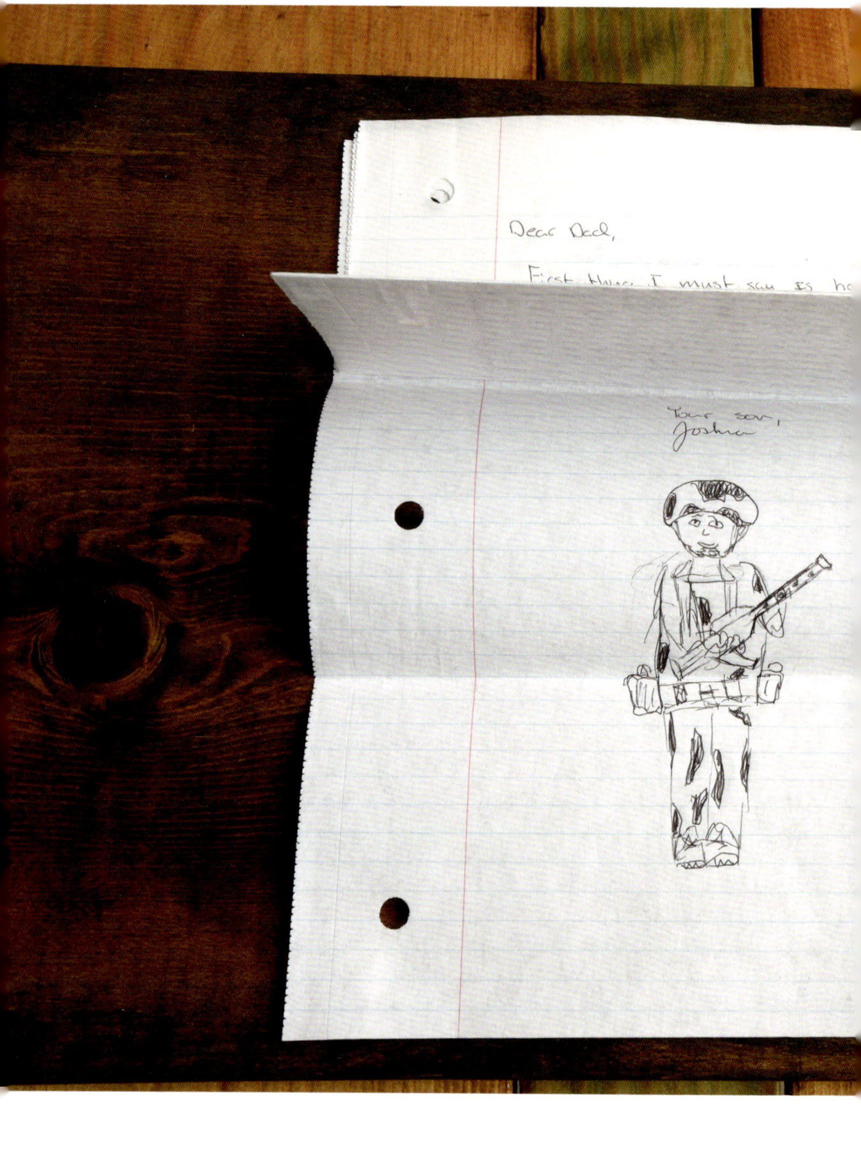
Dear Dad,
Your son,
Joshua

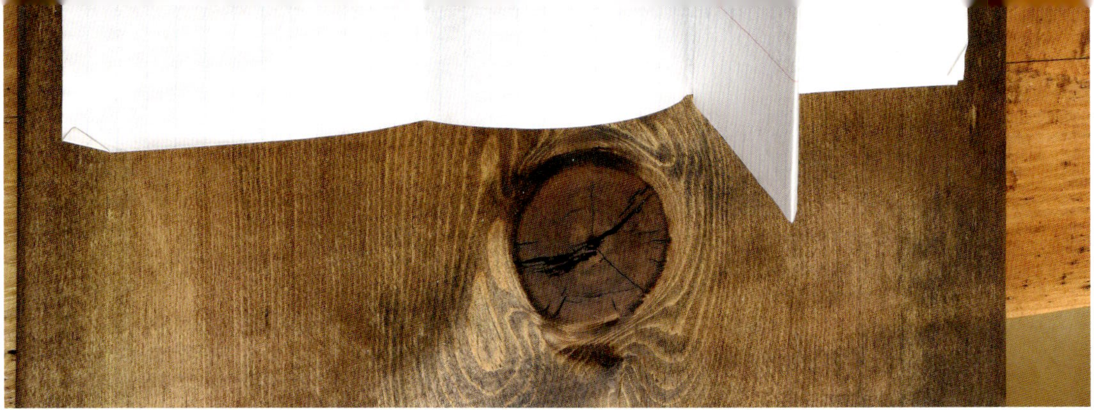

# HAGER

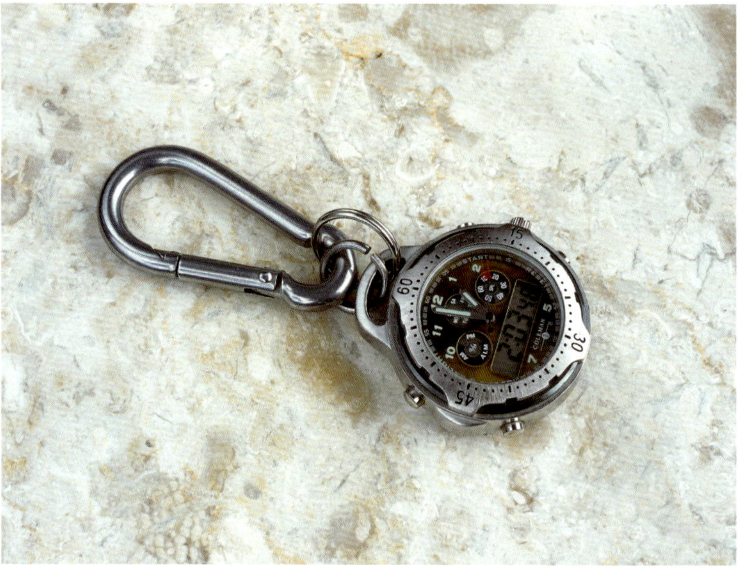
15
30
45
60
START
COLEMAN

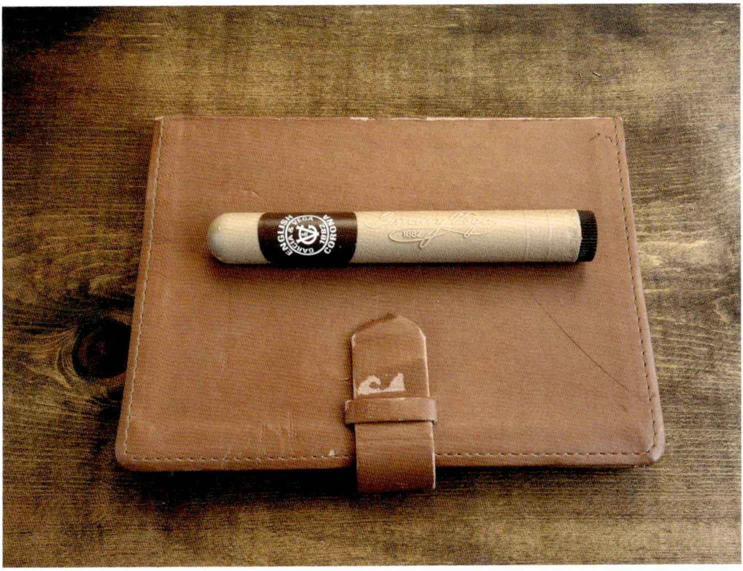
ENGLISH CORONA
GARCIA & VEGA
1882

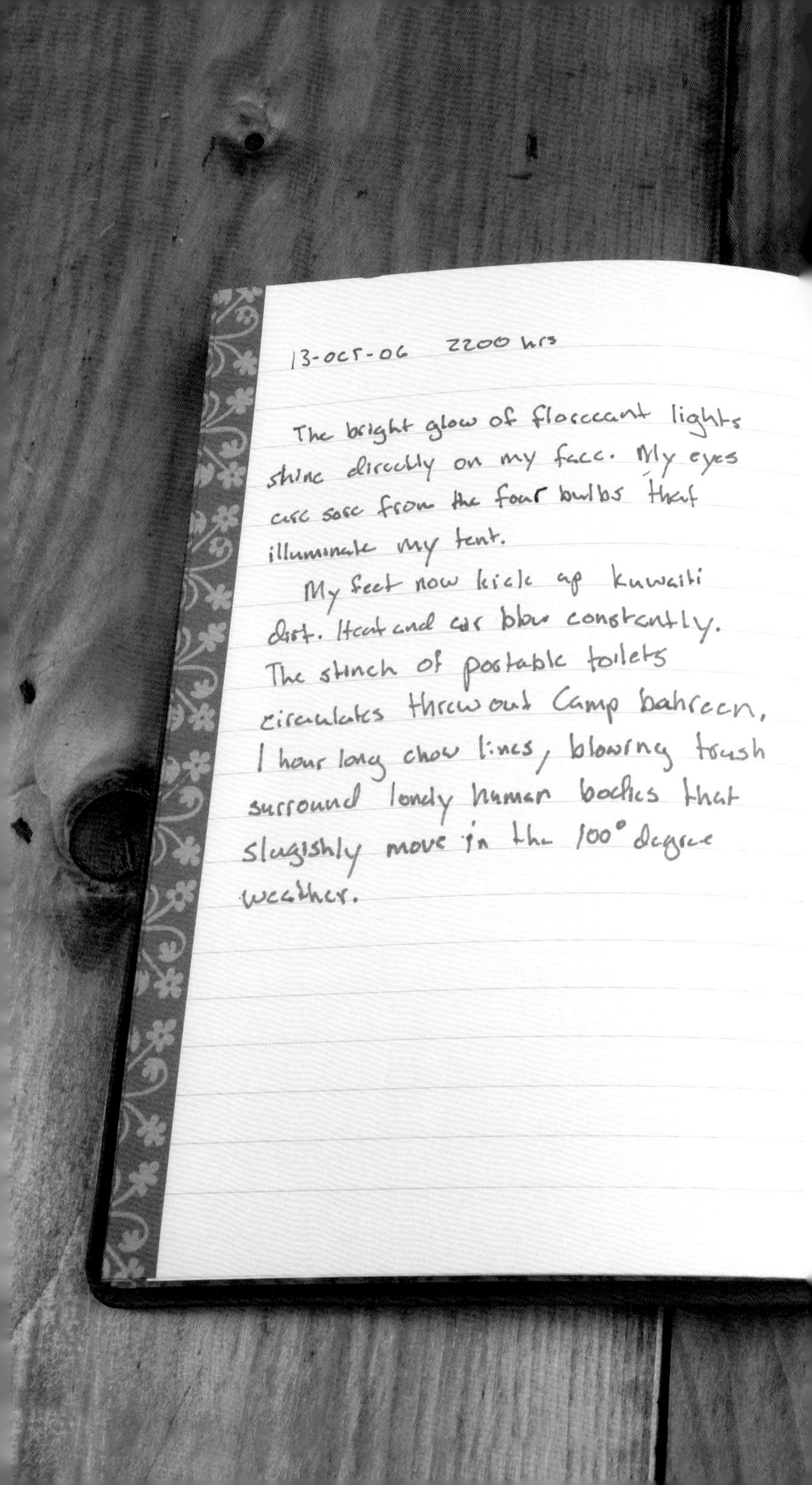

13-OCT-06 2200 hrs

The bright glow of floreccant lights shine directly on my face. My eyes are sore from the four bulbs that illuminate my tent.

My feet now kick up kuwaiti dirt. Heat and air blow constantly. The stinch of portable toilets circulates threwout Camp bahreen, 1 hour long chow lines, blowing trash surround lonely human bodies that slugishly move in the 100° degree weather.

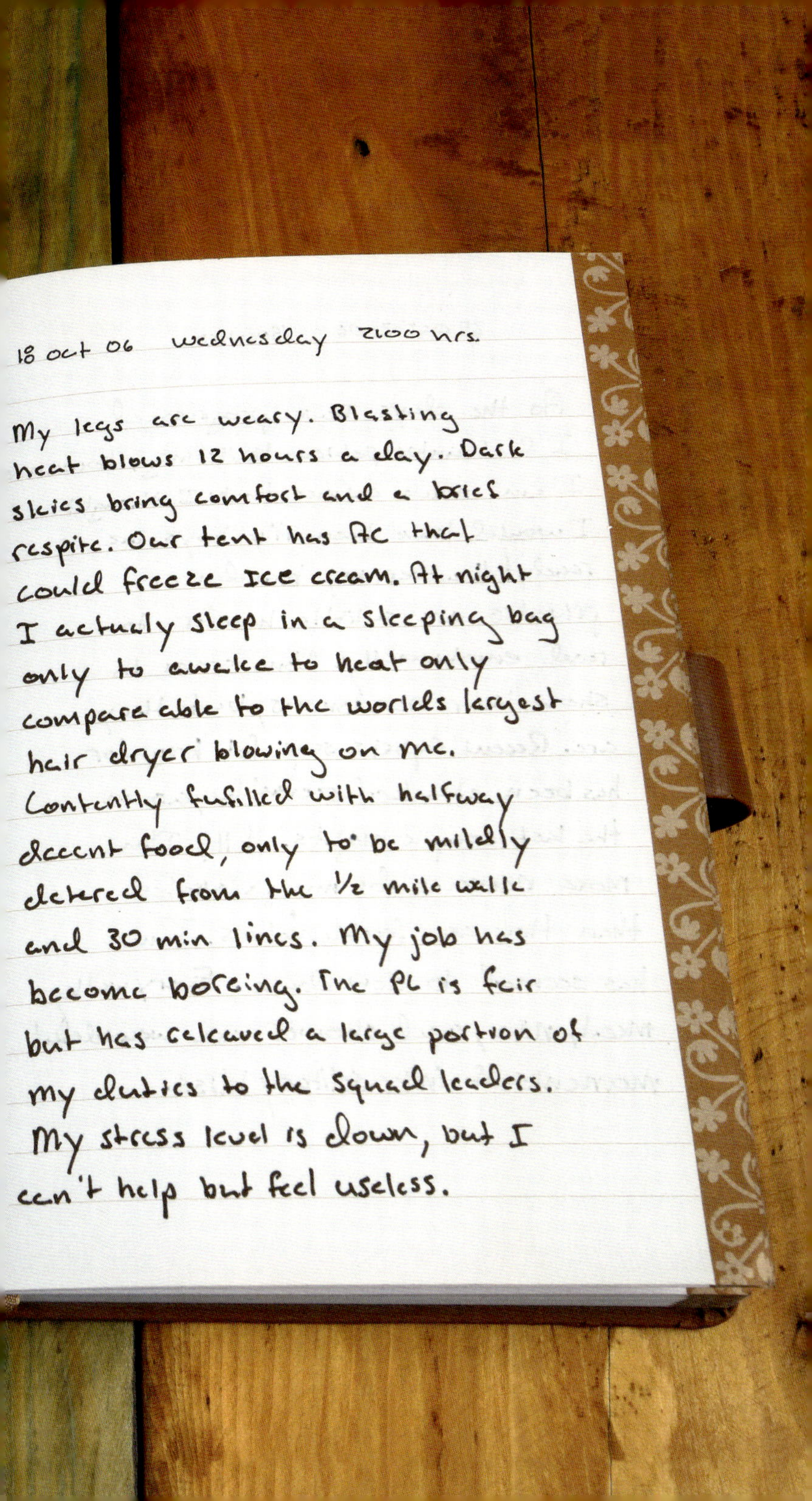
18 oct 06 wednesday 2100 hrs.
My legs are weary. Blasting
heat blows 12 hours a day. Dark
skies bring comfort and a brief
respite. Our tent has AC that
could freeze Ice cream. At night
I actualy sleep in a sleeping bag
only to awake to heat only
compare able to the worlds largest
hair dryer blowing on me.
Contently fufilled with halfway
decent food, only to be mildly
detered from the 1/2 mile walk
and 30 min lines. My job has
become boreing. The PL is fair
but has releaved a large portion of
my duties to the squad leaders.
My stress level is down, but I
can't help but feel useless.

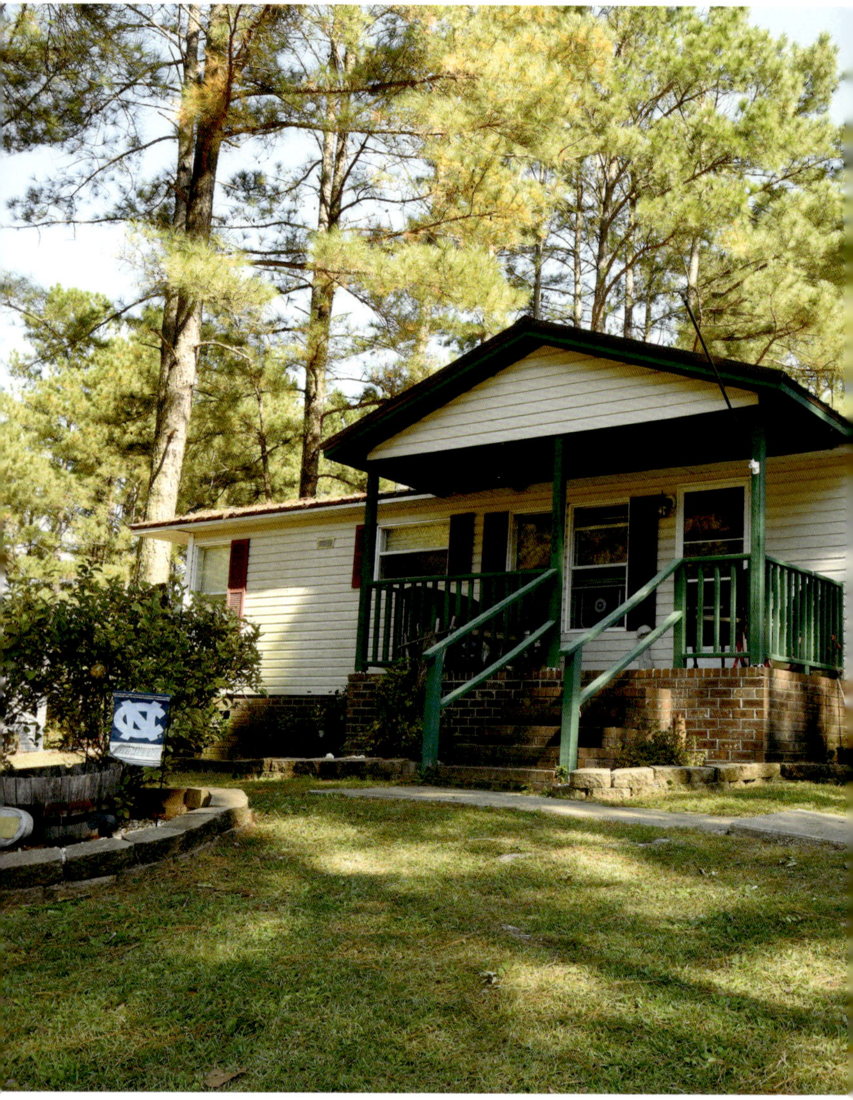

# JOHNSON

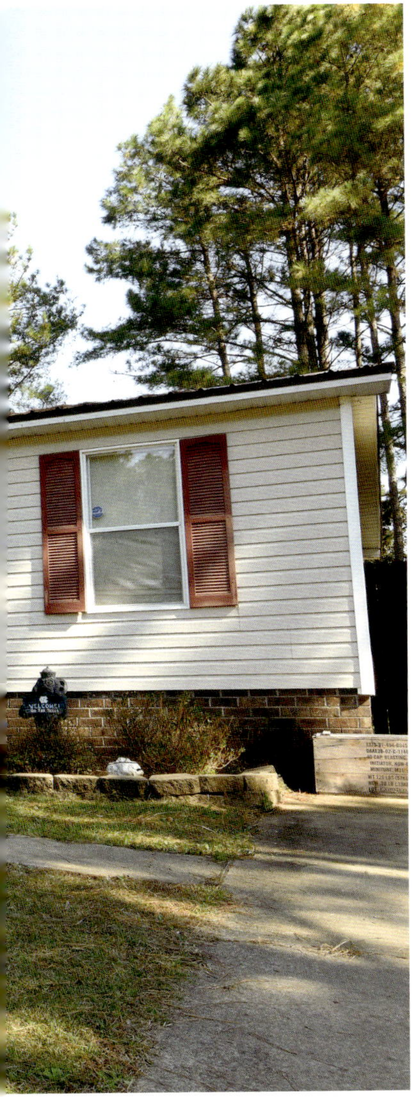

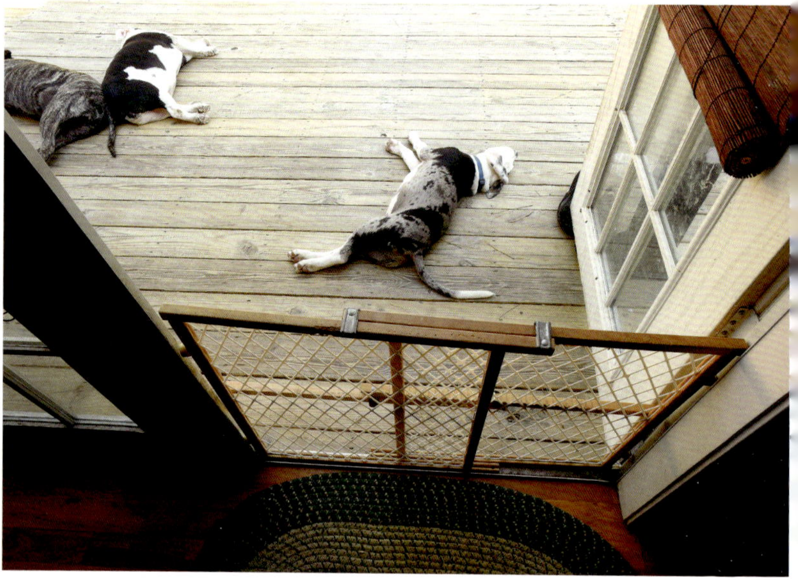

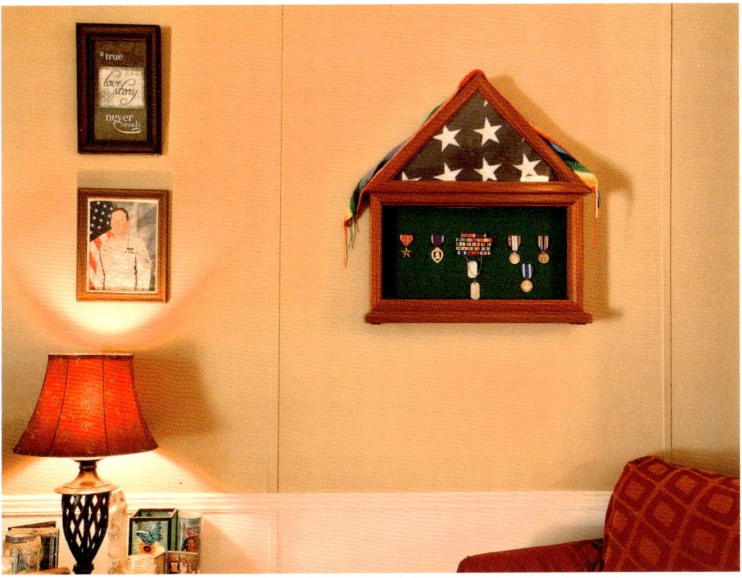
a true
love story
never ends

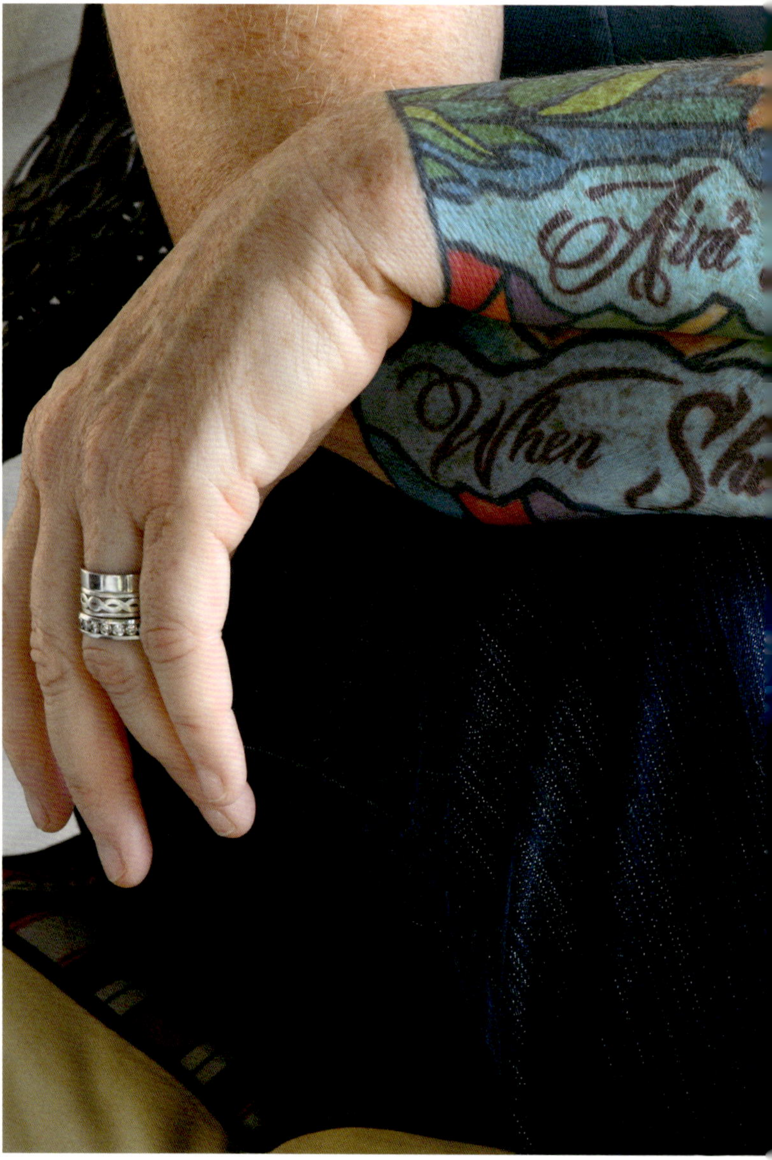
Ain't
When

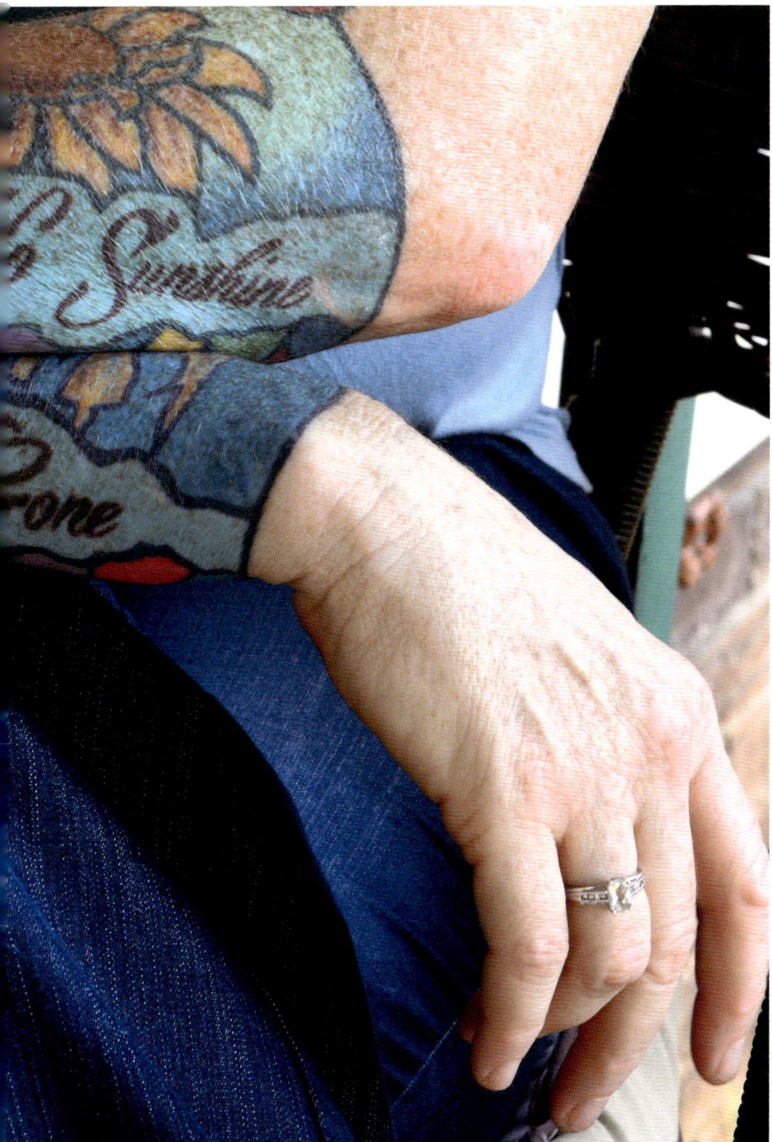
Sunshine

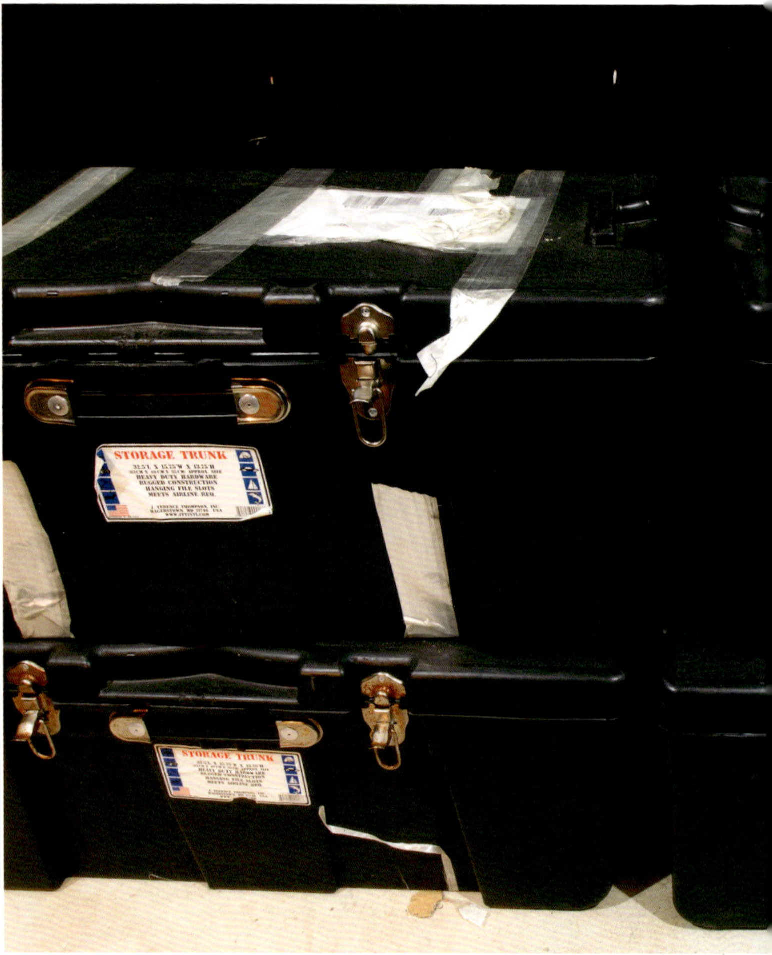
STORAGE TRUNK
HEAVY DUTY HARDWARE
RUGGED CONSTRUCTION
HANGING FILE SLOTS
MEETS AIRLINE REQ.
STORAGE TRUNK

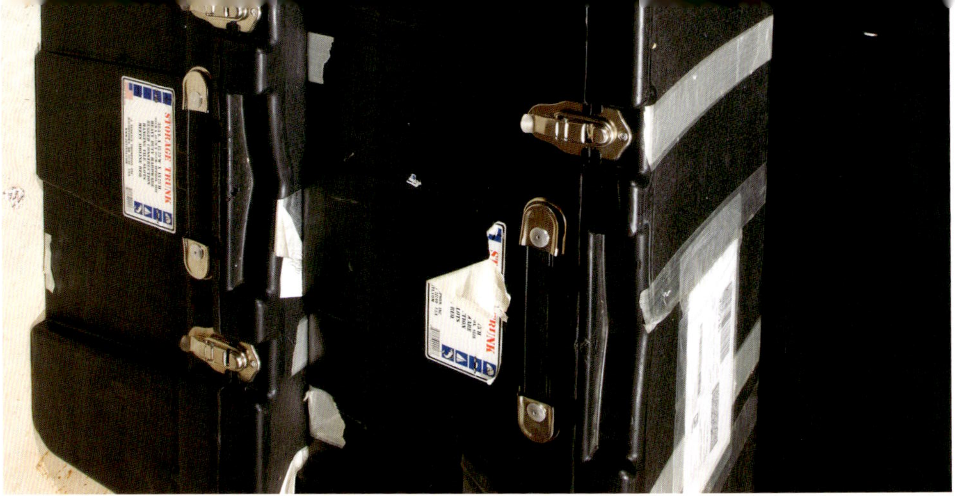


# LAKE

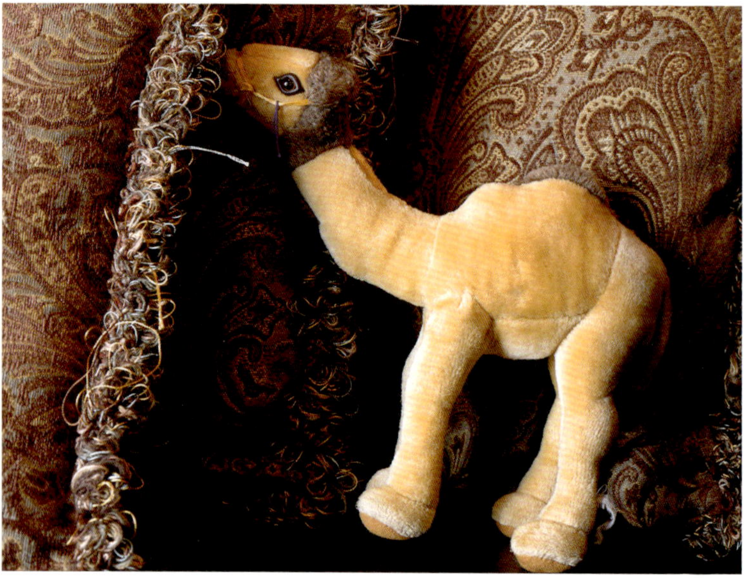

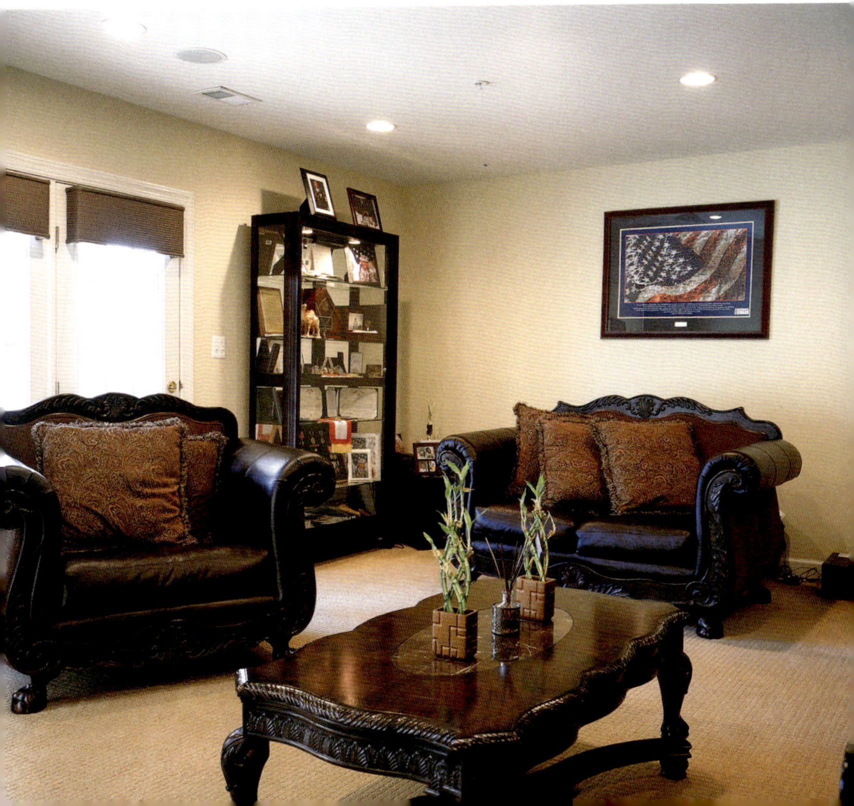

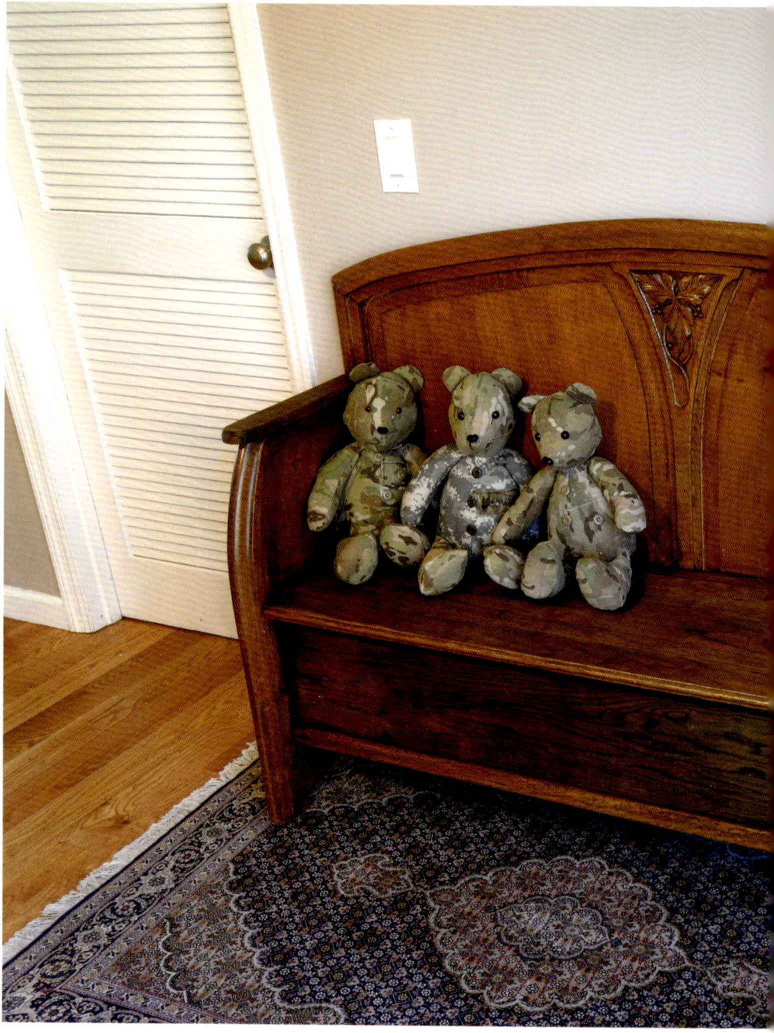

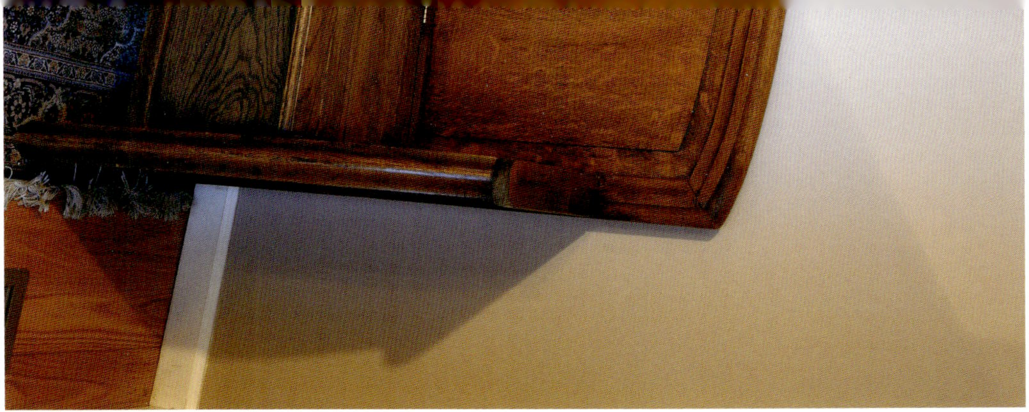

# LEONARD

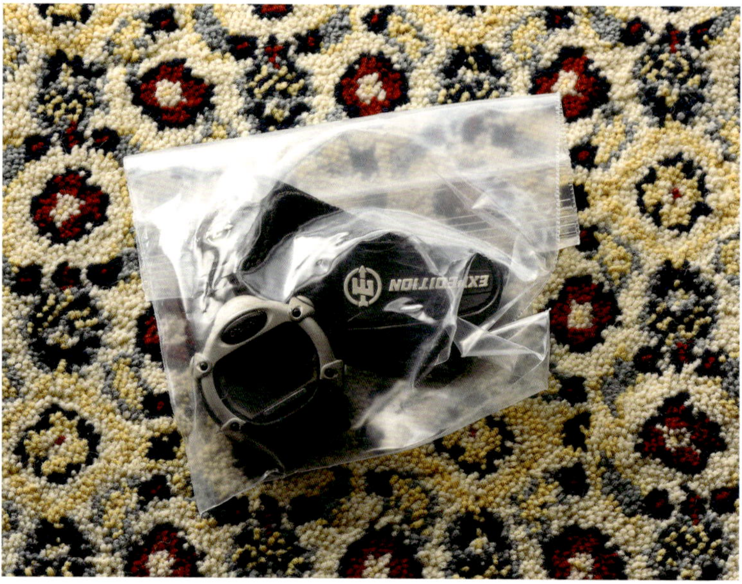

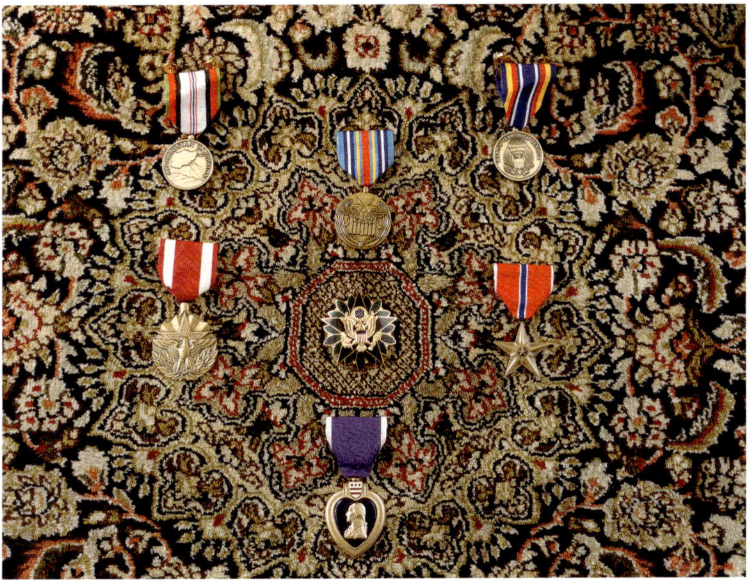

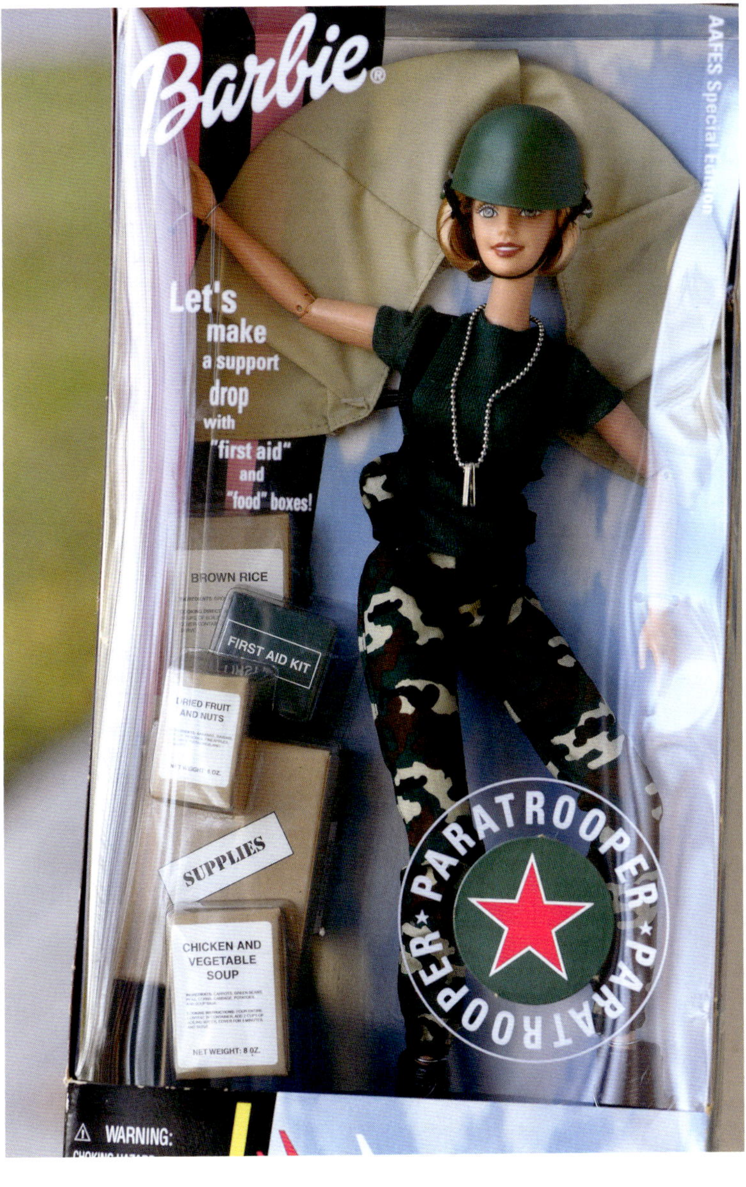
Barbie®
AAFES Special Edition
Let's make a support drop with "first aid" and "food" boxes!
BROWN RICE
FIRST AID KIT
DRIED FRUIT AND NUTS
SUPPLIES
CHICKEN AND VEGETABLE SOUP
NET WEIGHT: 8 OZ.
PARATROOPER ★ PARATROOPER ★
WARNING:

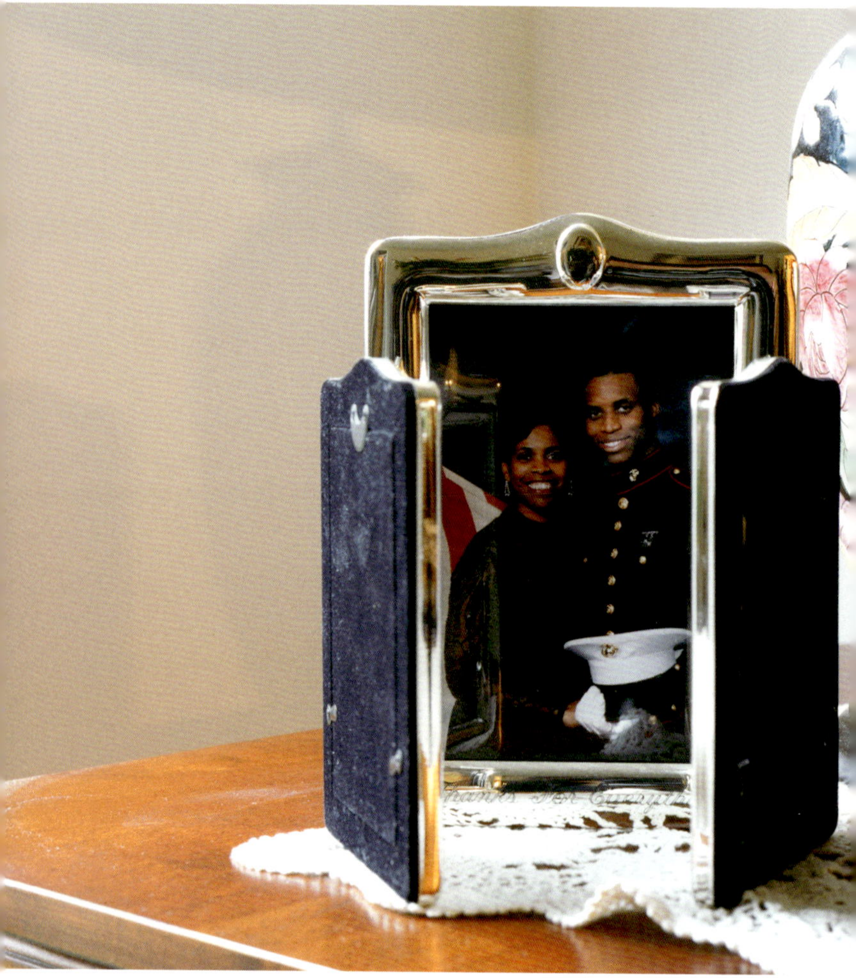

# MELTON

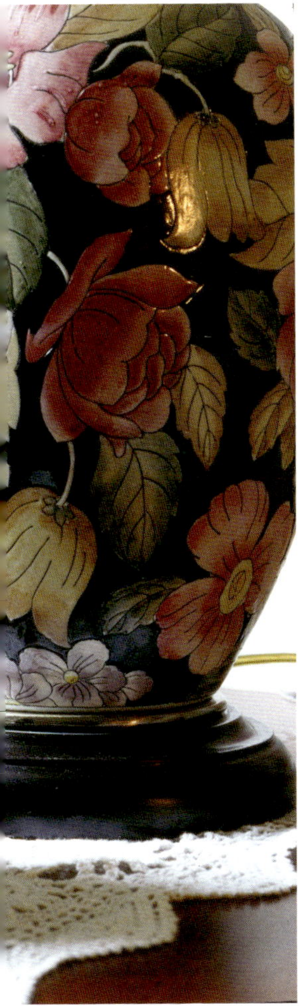

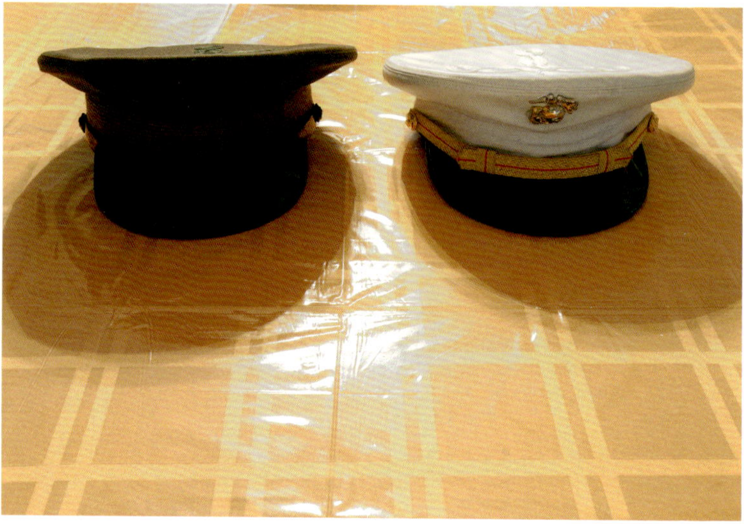

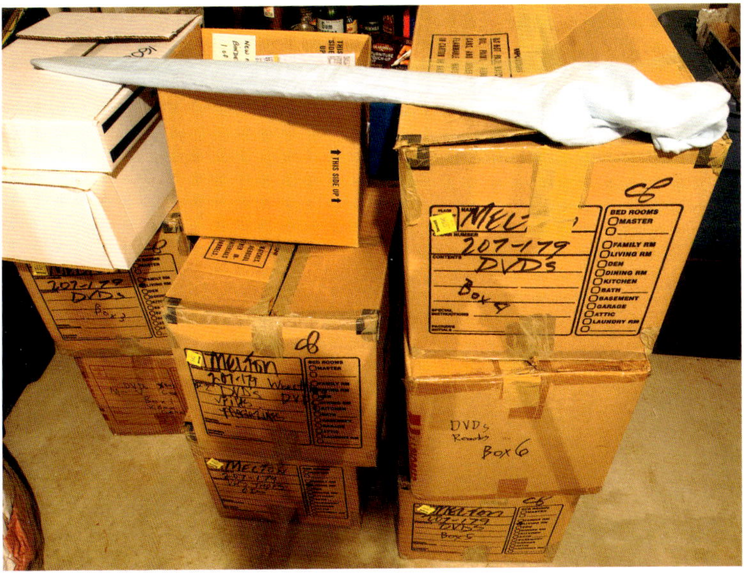
THIS SIDE UP
BED ROOMS
MASTER
FAMILY RM
LIVING RM
DEN
DINING RM
KITCHEN
BATH
BASEMENT
GARAGE
ATTIC
LAUNDRY RM
207-179
DVDs
Melton
DVDs
Box 6

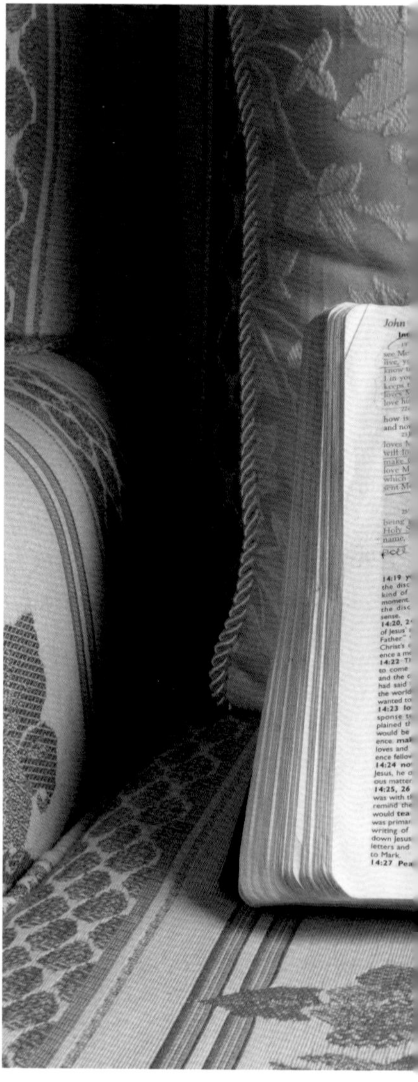

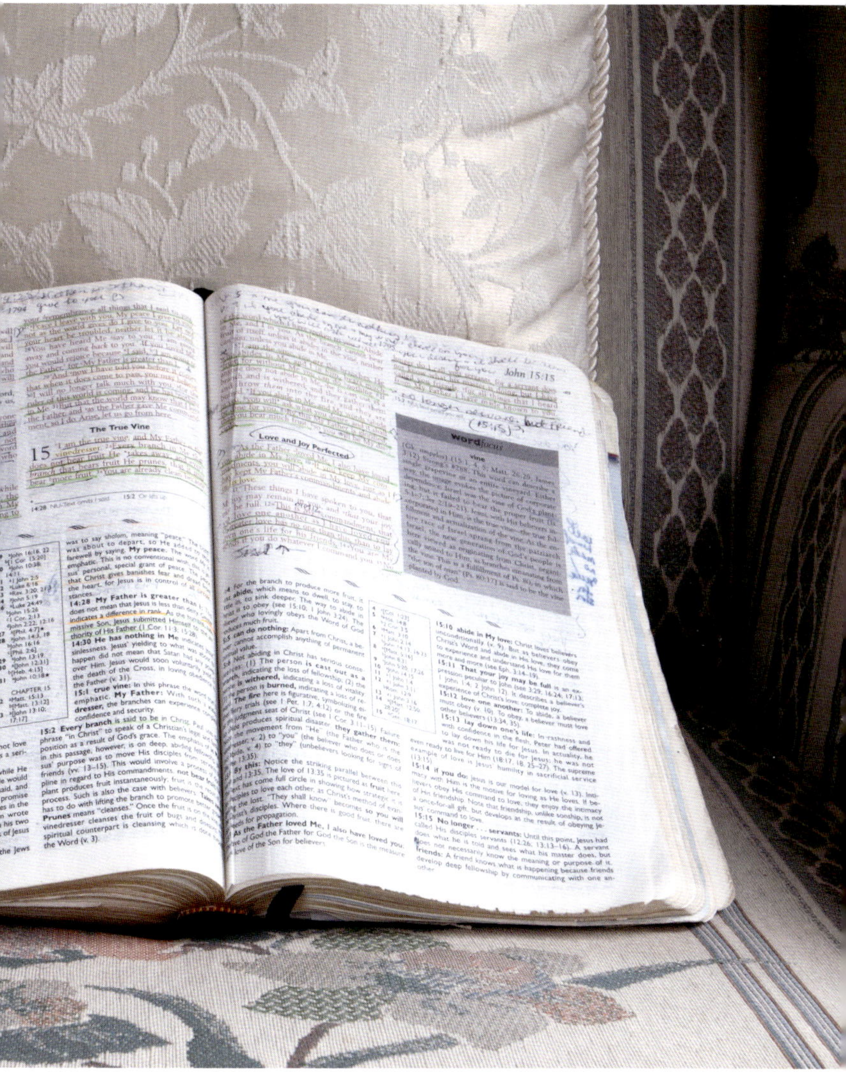
The True Vine
Love and Joy Perfected
John 15:15
vine

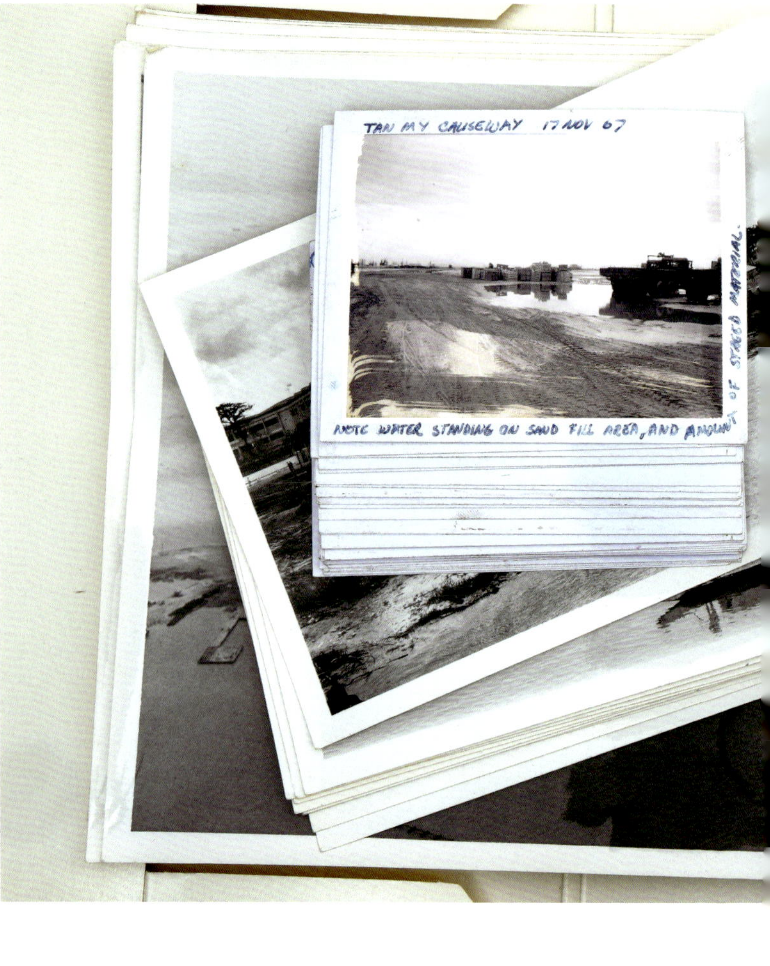
TAN MY CAUSEWAY 17 NOV 67
NOTE WATER STANDING ON SAND FILL AREA, AND AMOUNT OF STAGED MATERIAL.

# MOINESTER*

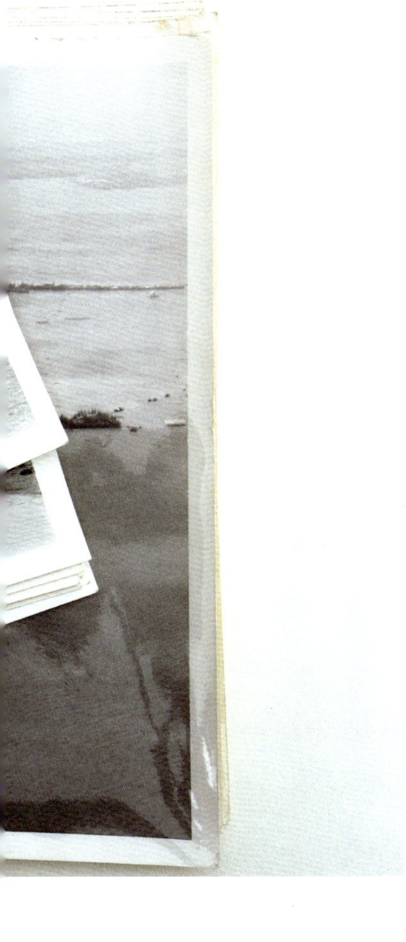

*Brother

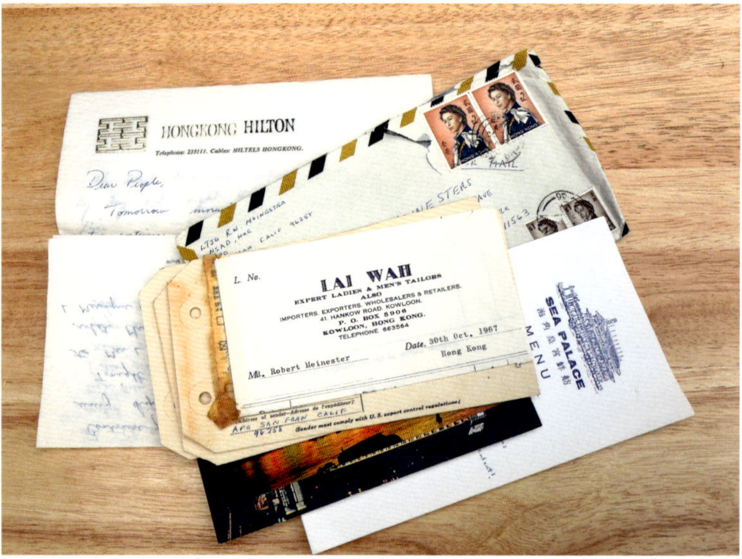
HONGKONG HILTON
Telephone: 233111. Cables: HILTELS HONGKONG.
Dear People,
Tomorrow
L. No.
LAI WAH
EXPERT LADIES & MEN'S TAILORS
ALSO
IMPORTERS, EXPORTERS, WHOLESALERS & RETAILERS.
41. HANKOW ROAD. KOWLOON.
P. O. BOX 5906
KOWLOON, HONG KONG.
TELEPHONE 663564
Date, 30th Oct. 1967
Hong Kong
Mr. Robert Meinester
(Sender must comply with U.S. export control regulations)
APO SAN FRAN CALIF
96258
SEA PALACE
MENU

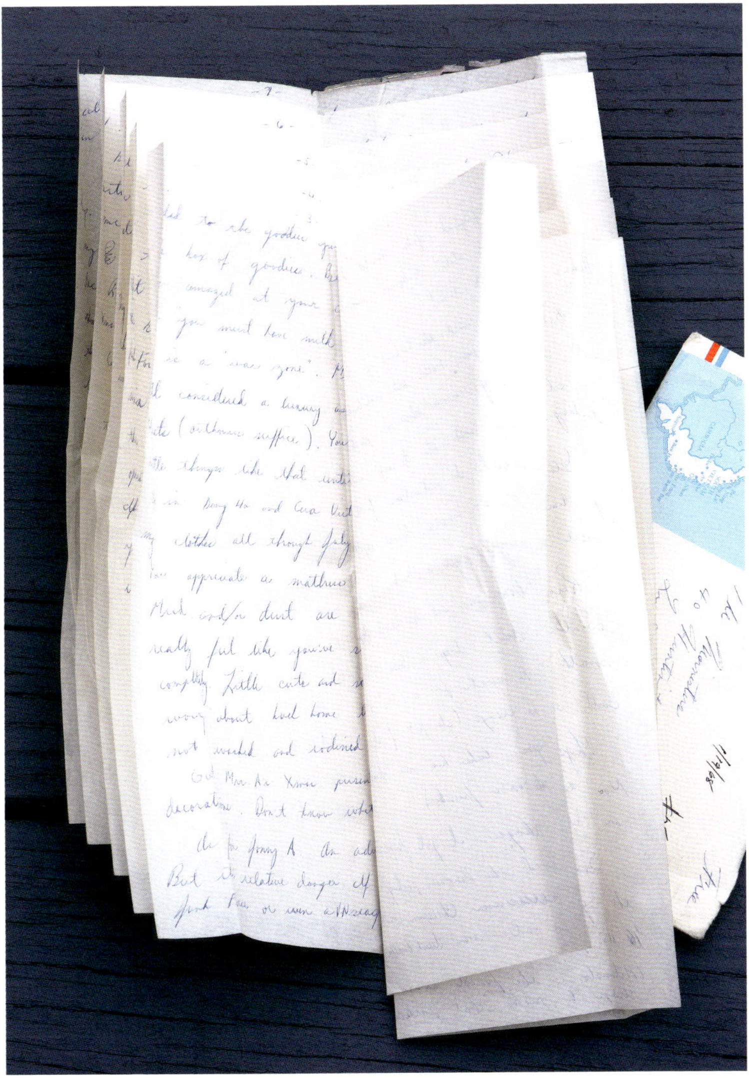

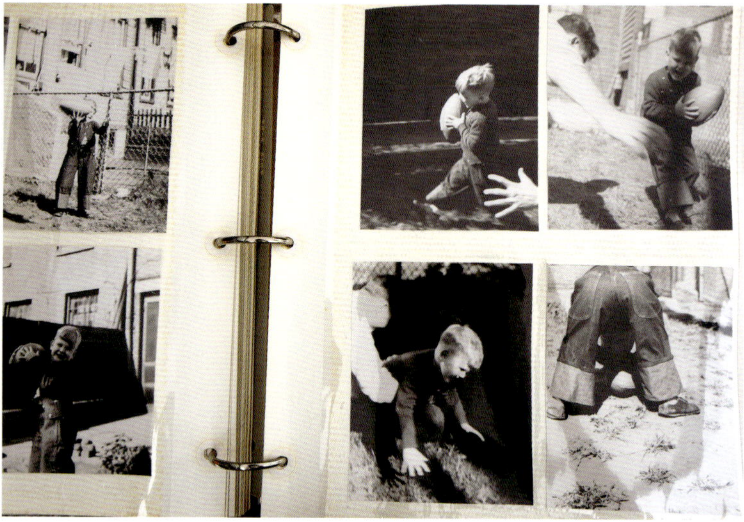

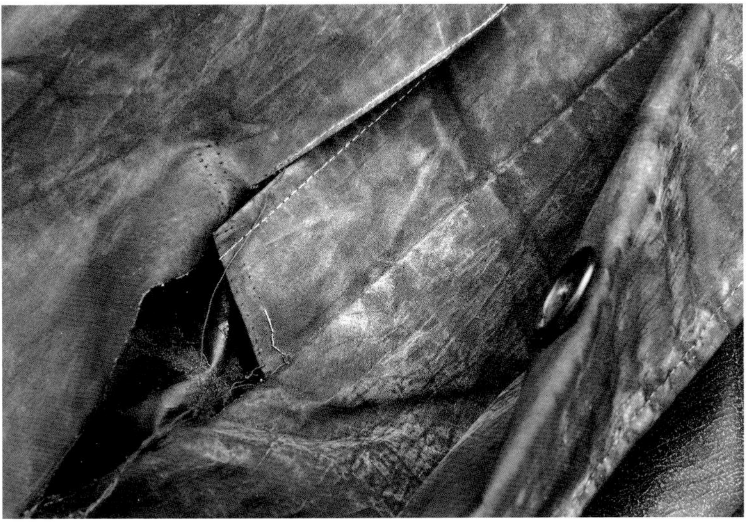

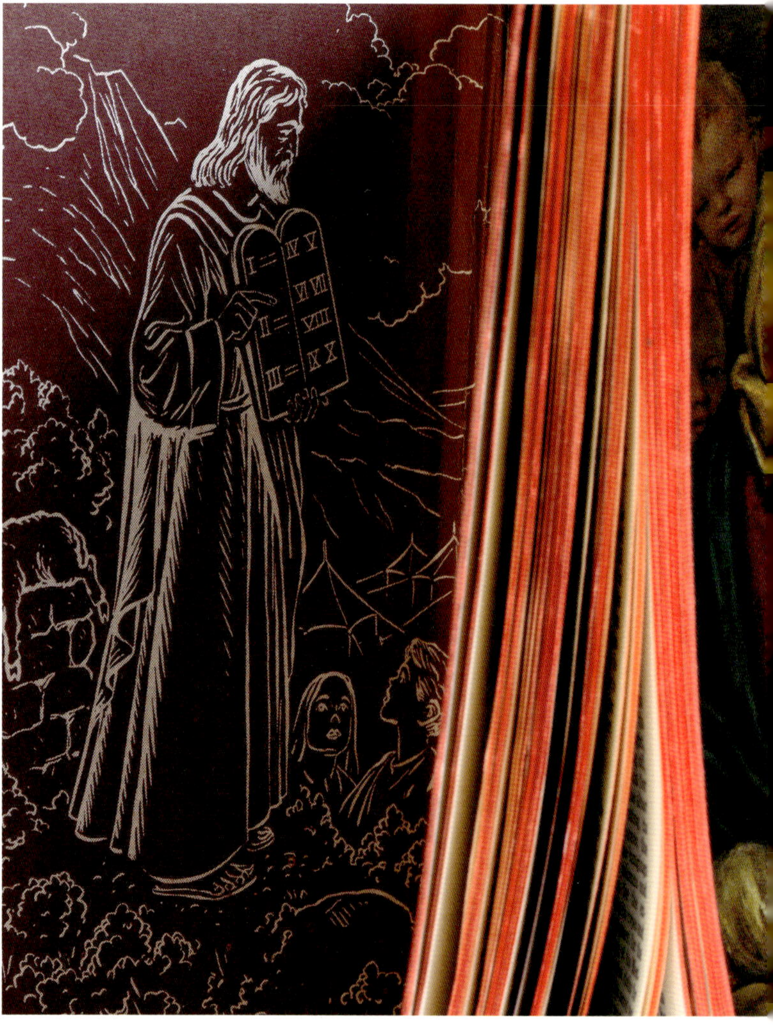

# MOINE STER*

*Sister

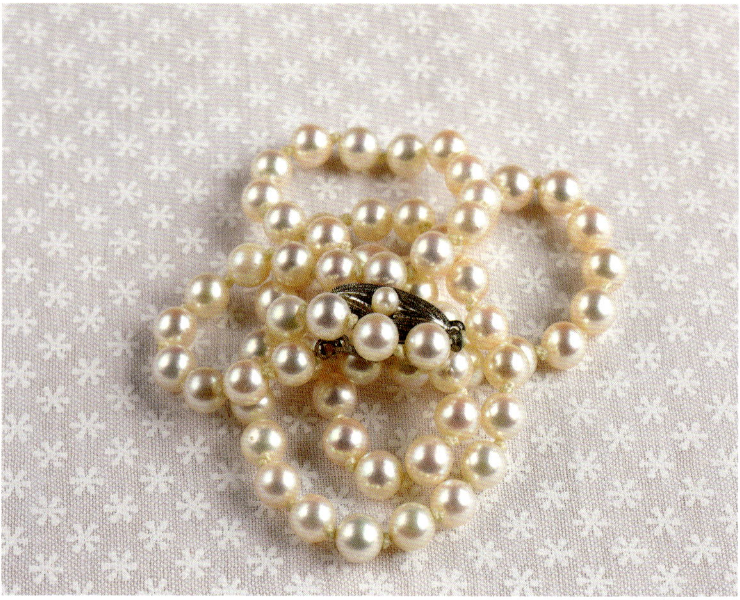

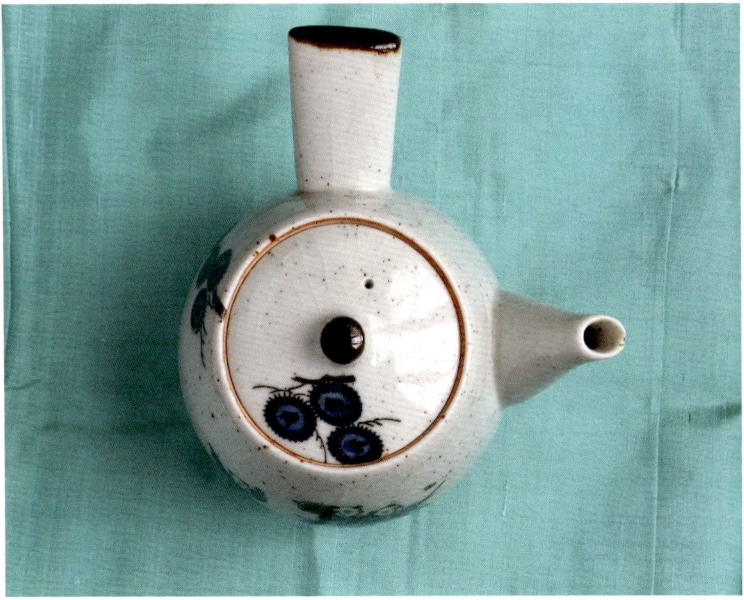

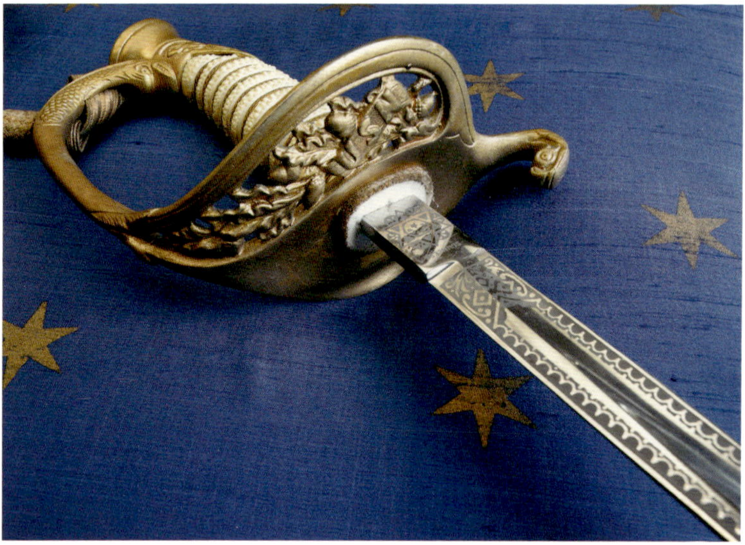

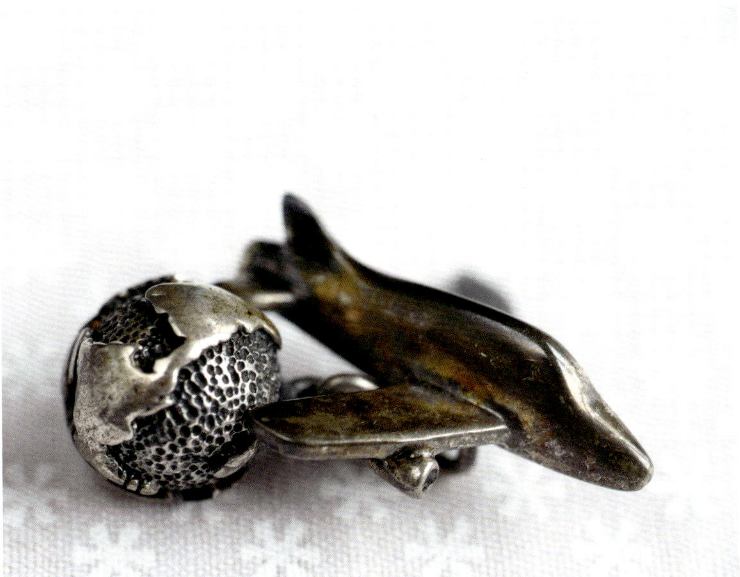

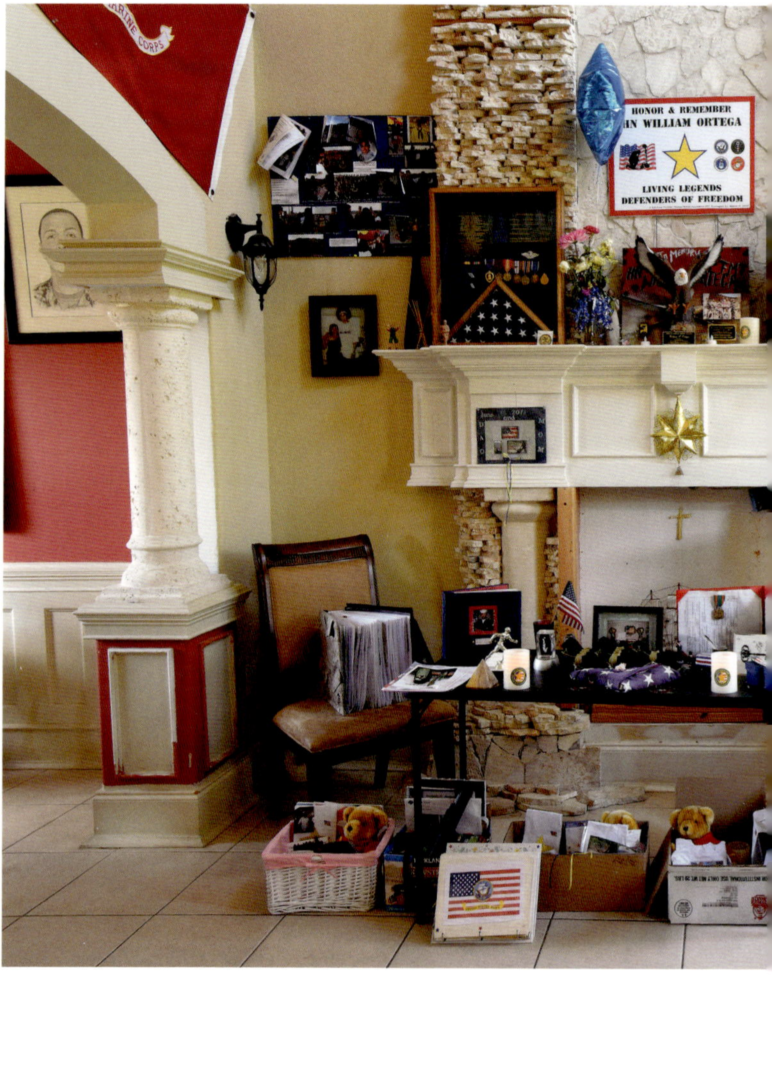
HONOR & REMEMBER
HN WILLIAM ORTEGA
LIVING LEGENDS
DEFENDERS OF FREEDOM

# ORTEGA

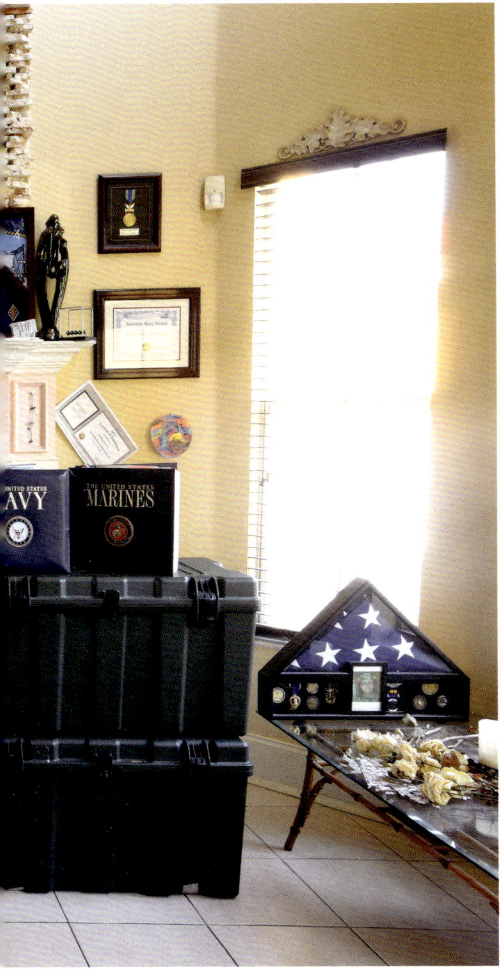

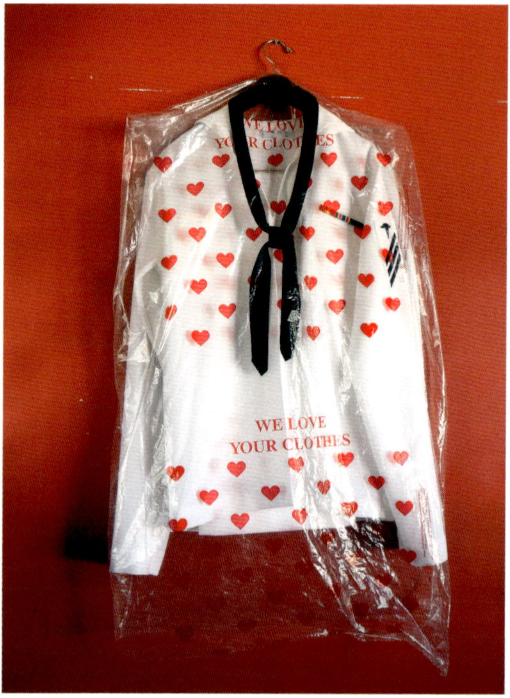
WE LOVE
YOUR CLOTHES
WE LOVE
YOUR CLOTHES

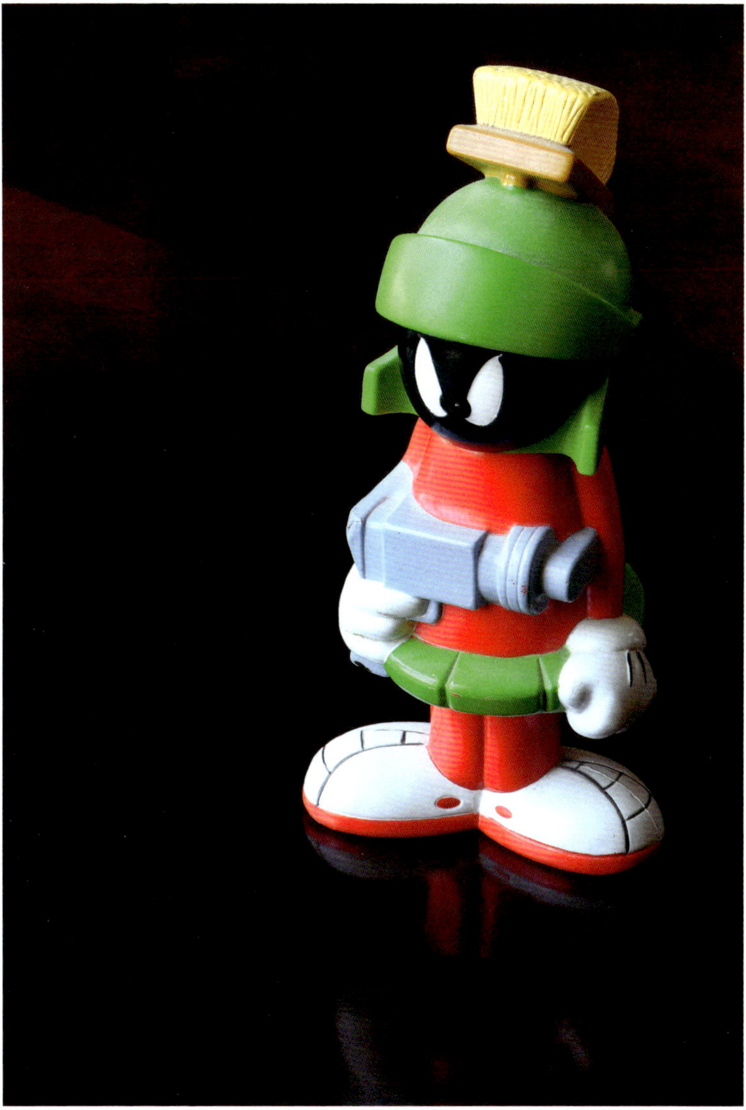

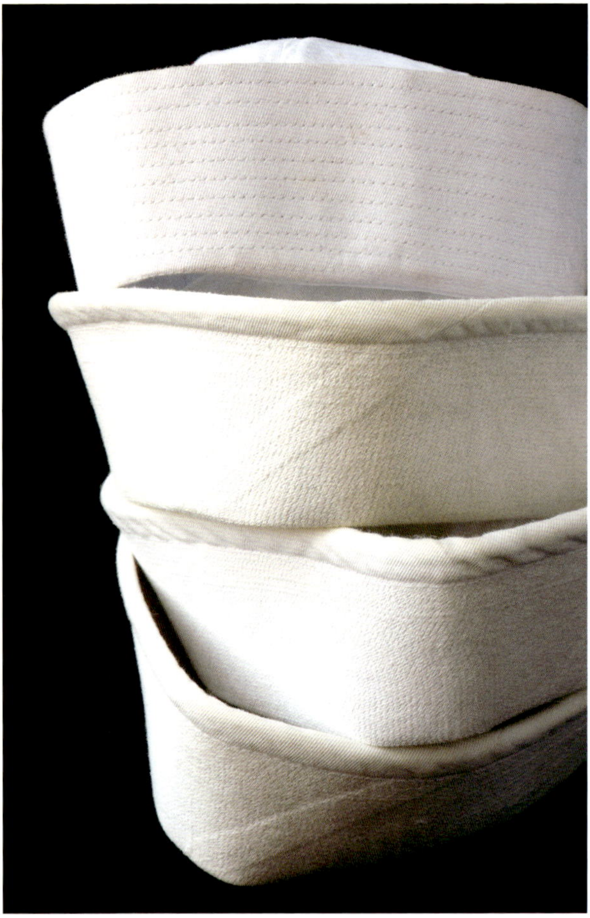

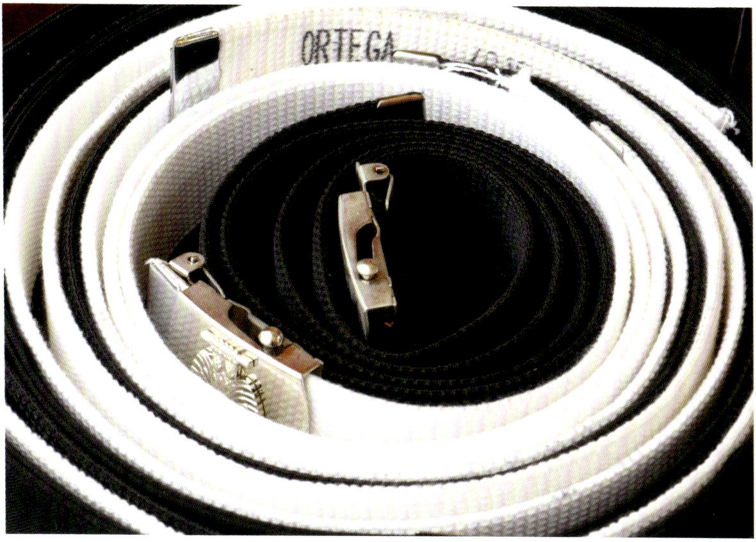
ORTEGA

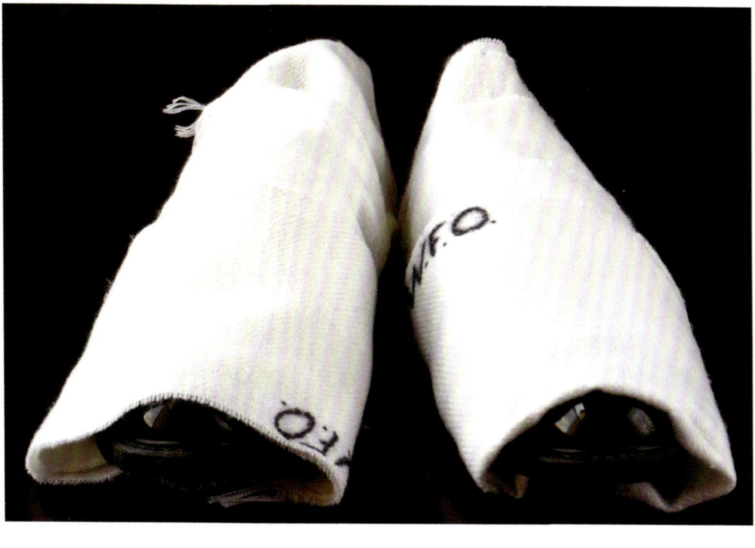

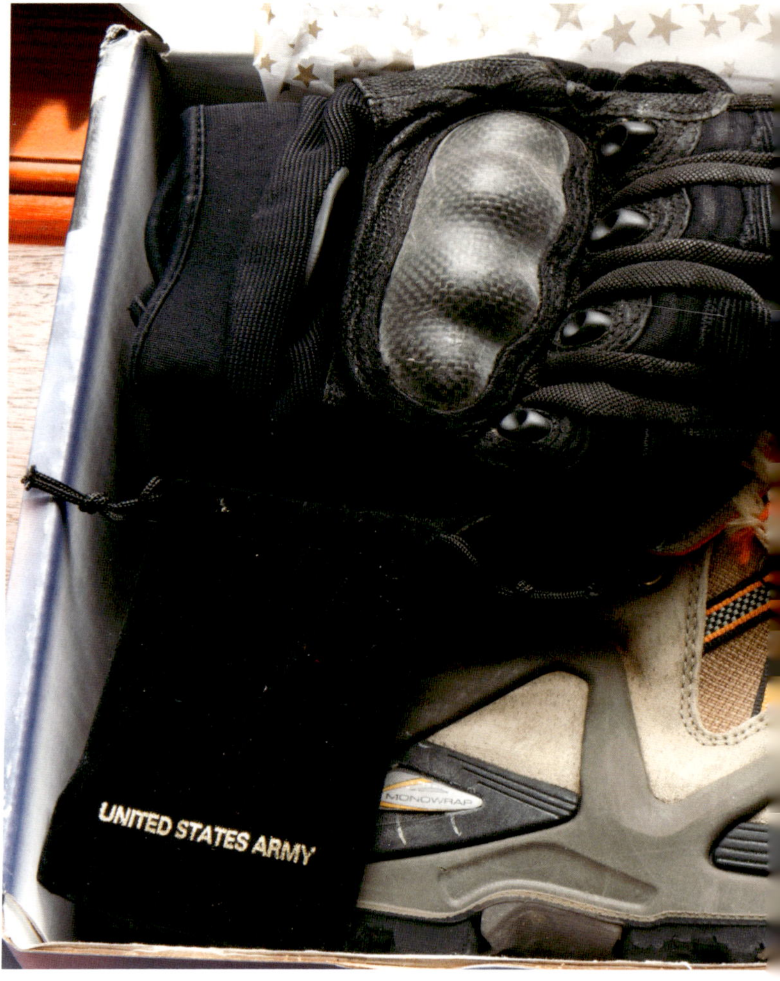
UNITED STATES ARMY
MONOWRAP

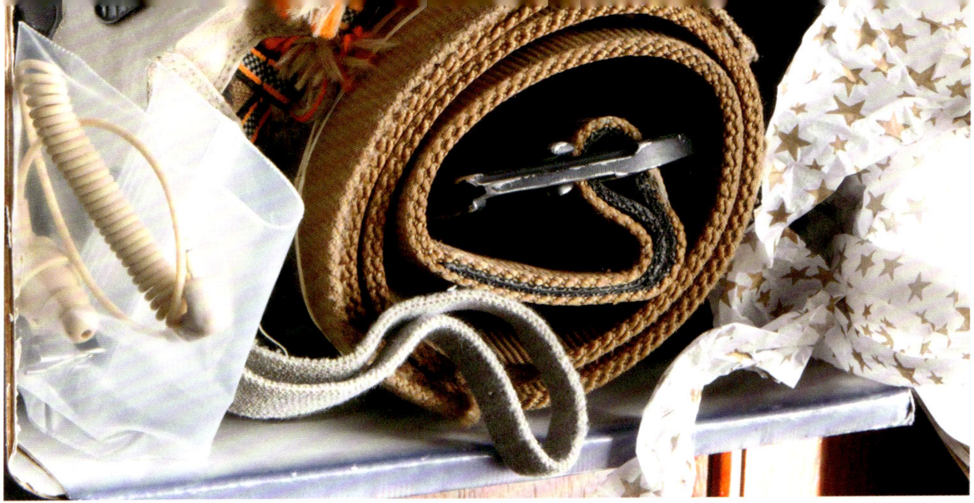

# OSBORN

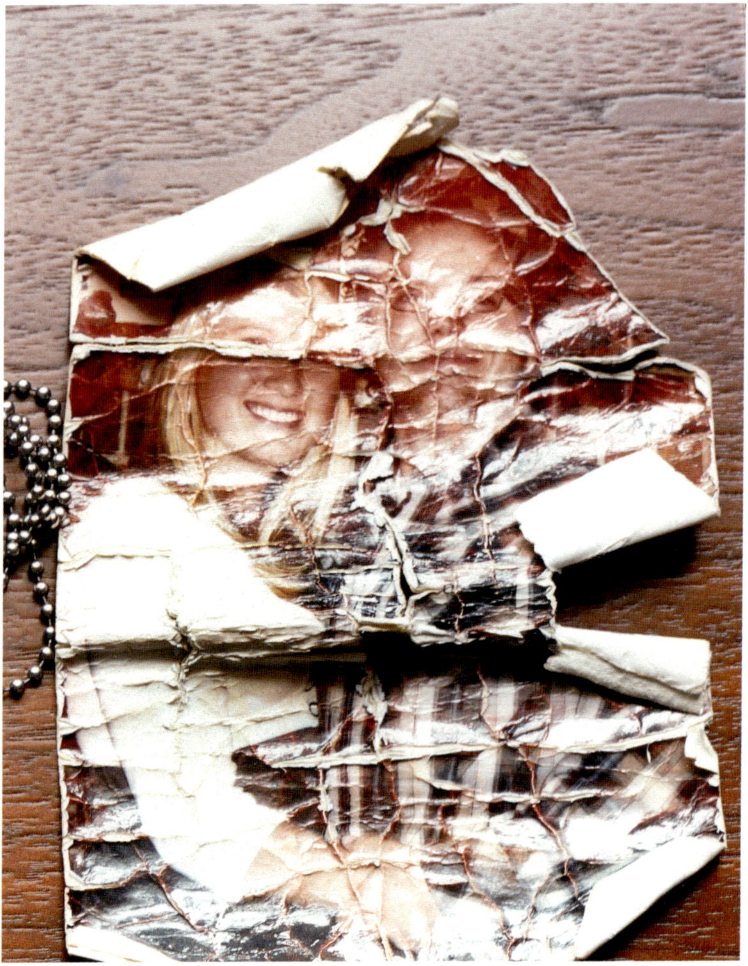

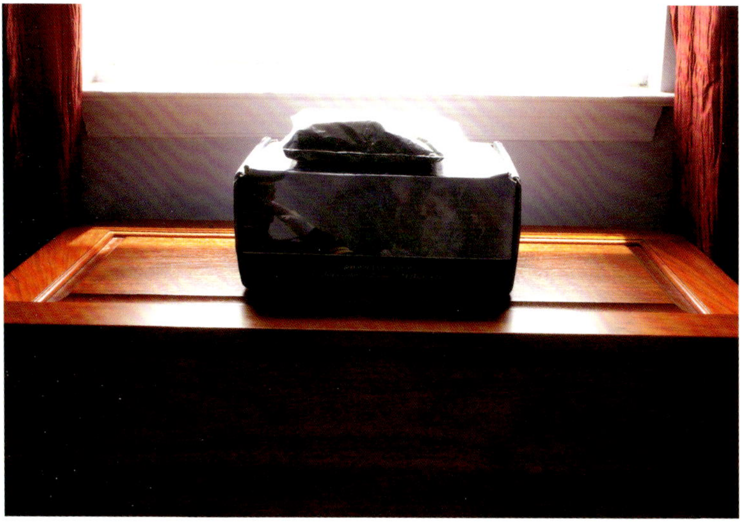

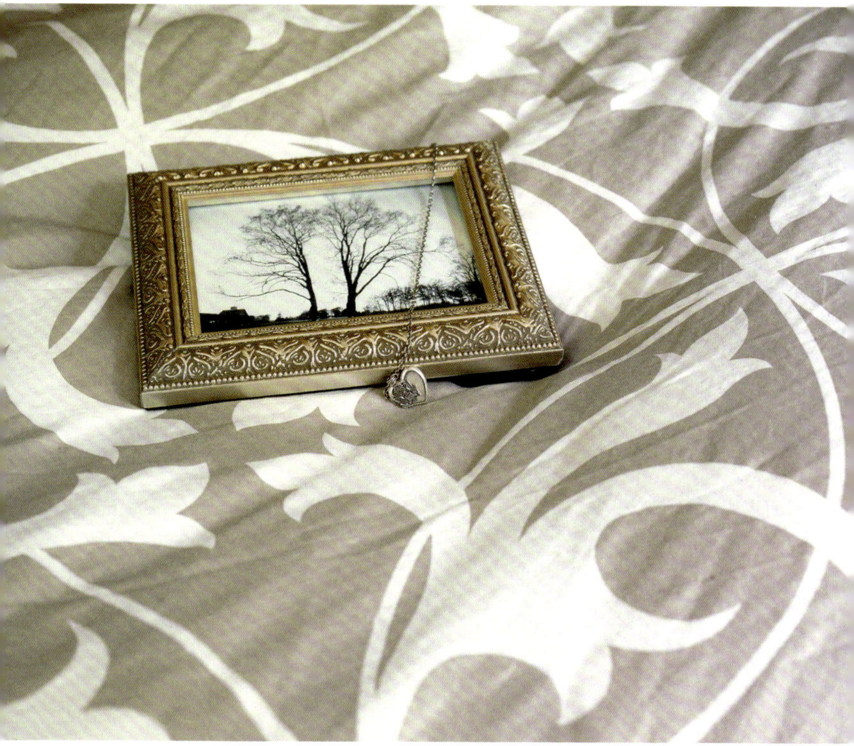

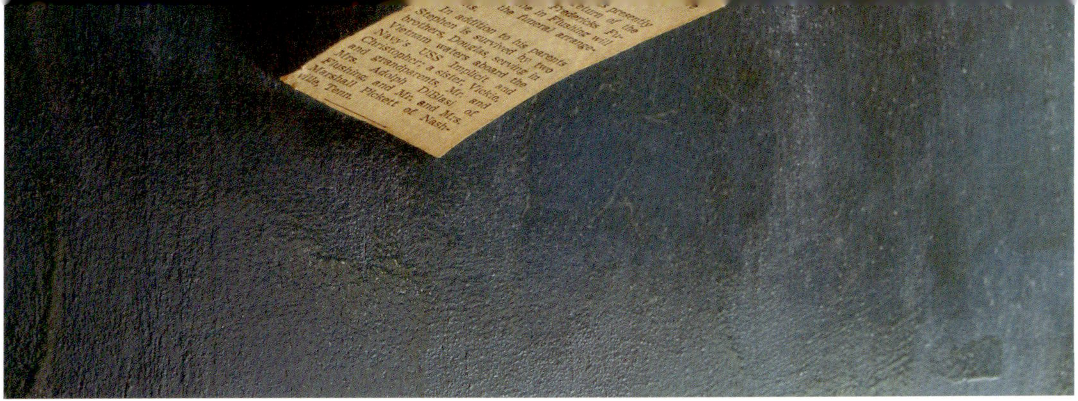
In addition to his parents
Stephen is survived by two
brothers, Douglas, serving in
Vietnam waters aboard the
Navy's USS Implicit, and
Christopher; a sister, Vickie,
and grandparents, Mr. and
Mrs. Adolph DiBlasi of
Flushing, and Mr. and Mrs.
Marshall Pickett of Nash-
ville, Tenn.

# PICKETT

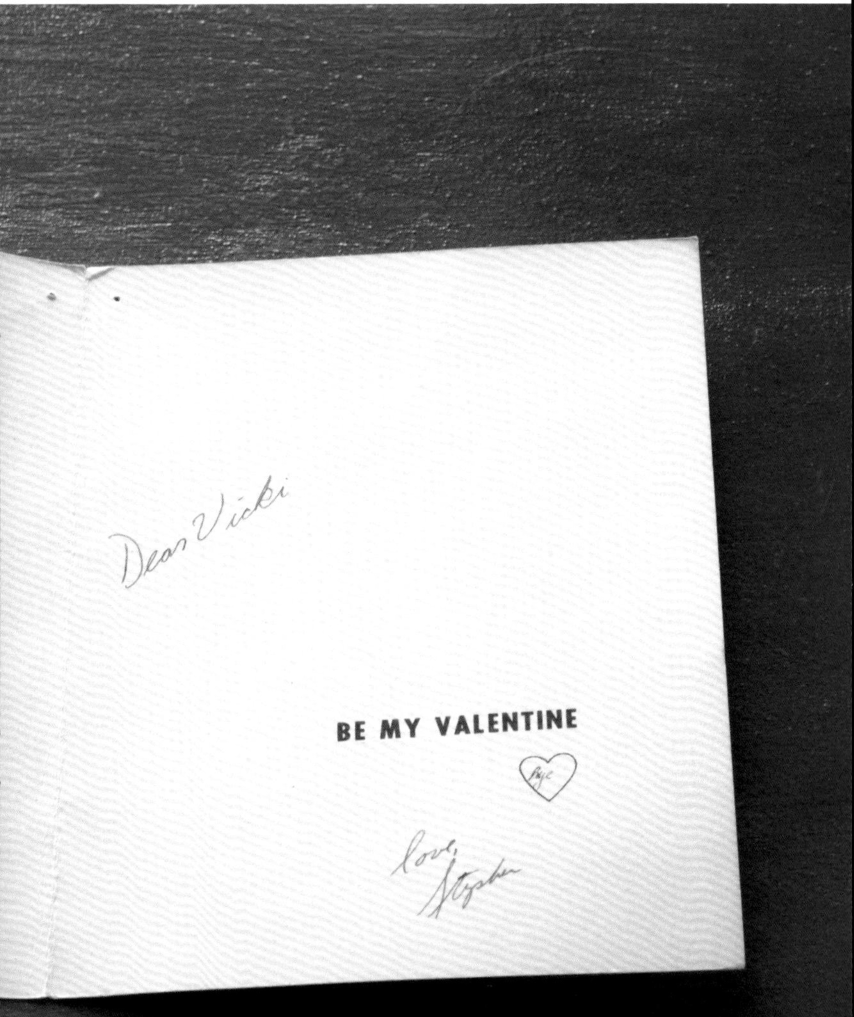
Dear Vicki
BE MY VALENTINE
love,
Stephen

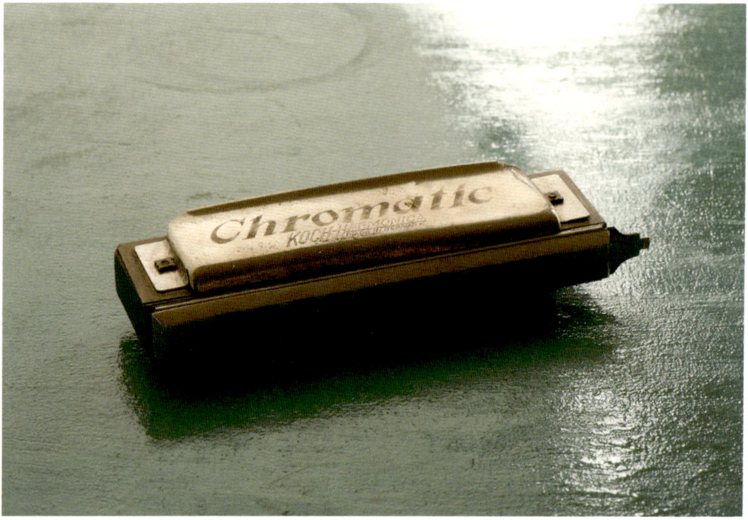
Chromatic

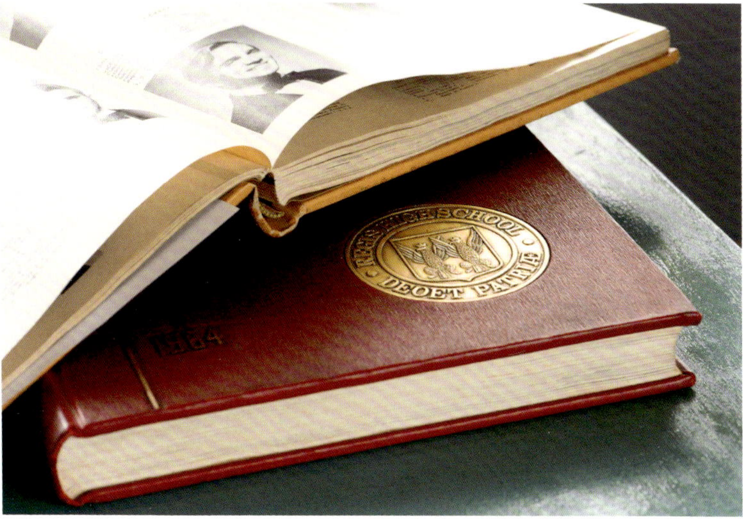

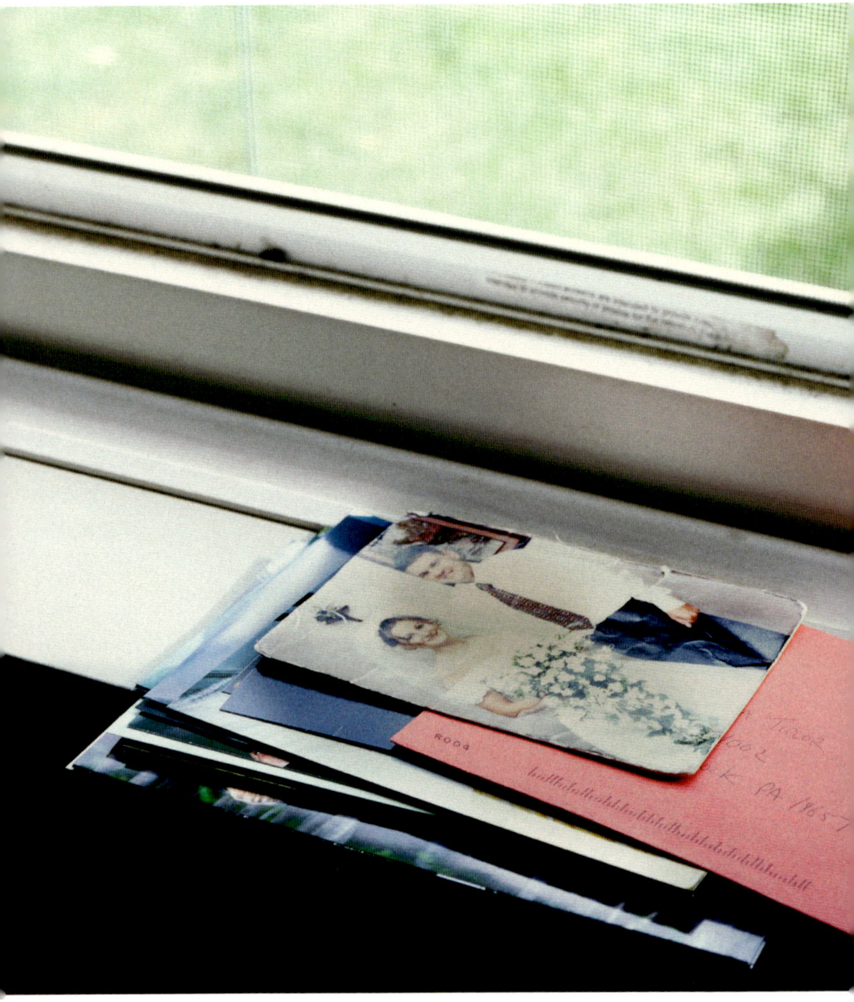

# TUDOR

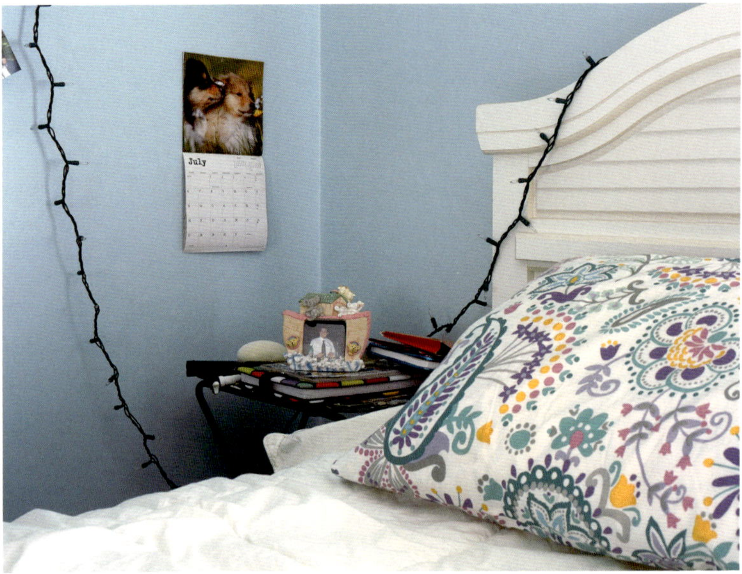
July

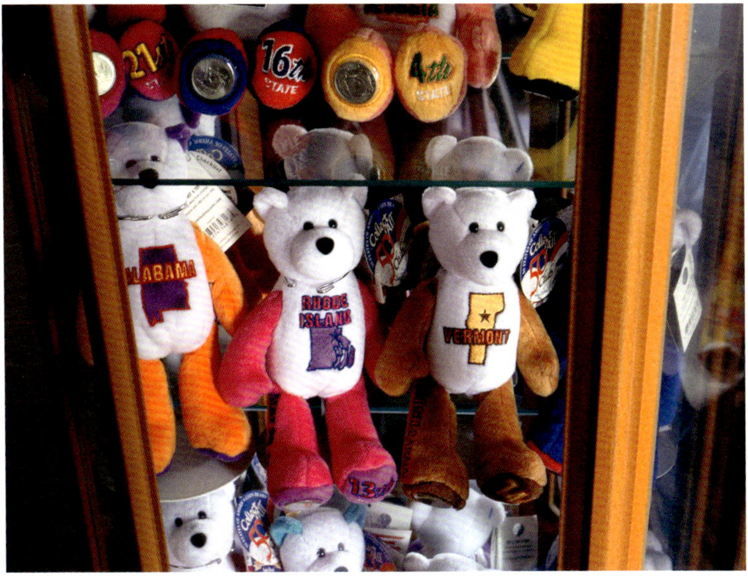
16th
STATE
4th
STATE
RHODE
ISLAND
VERMONT

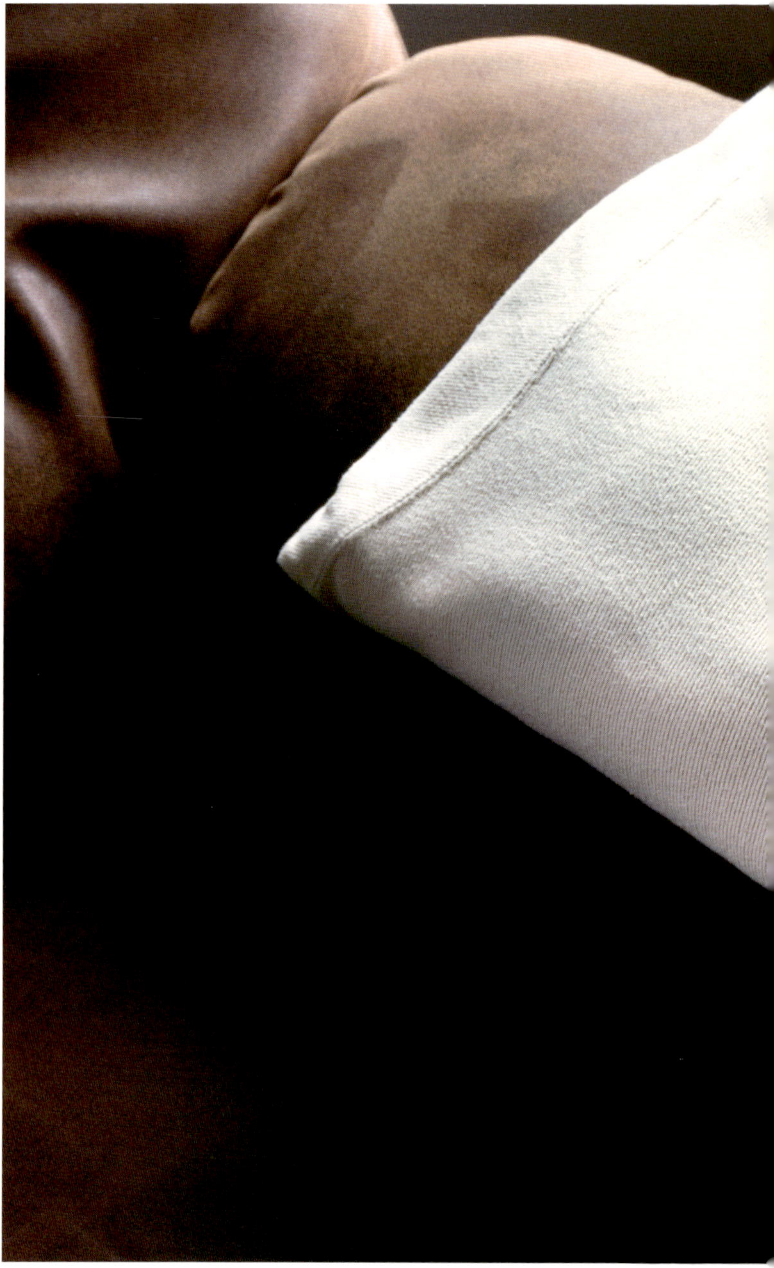

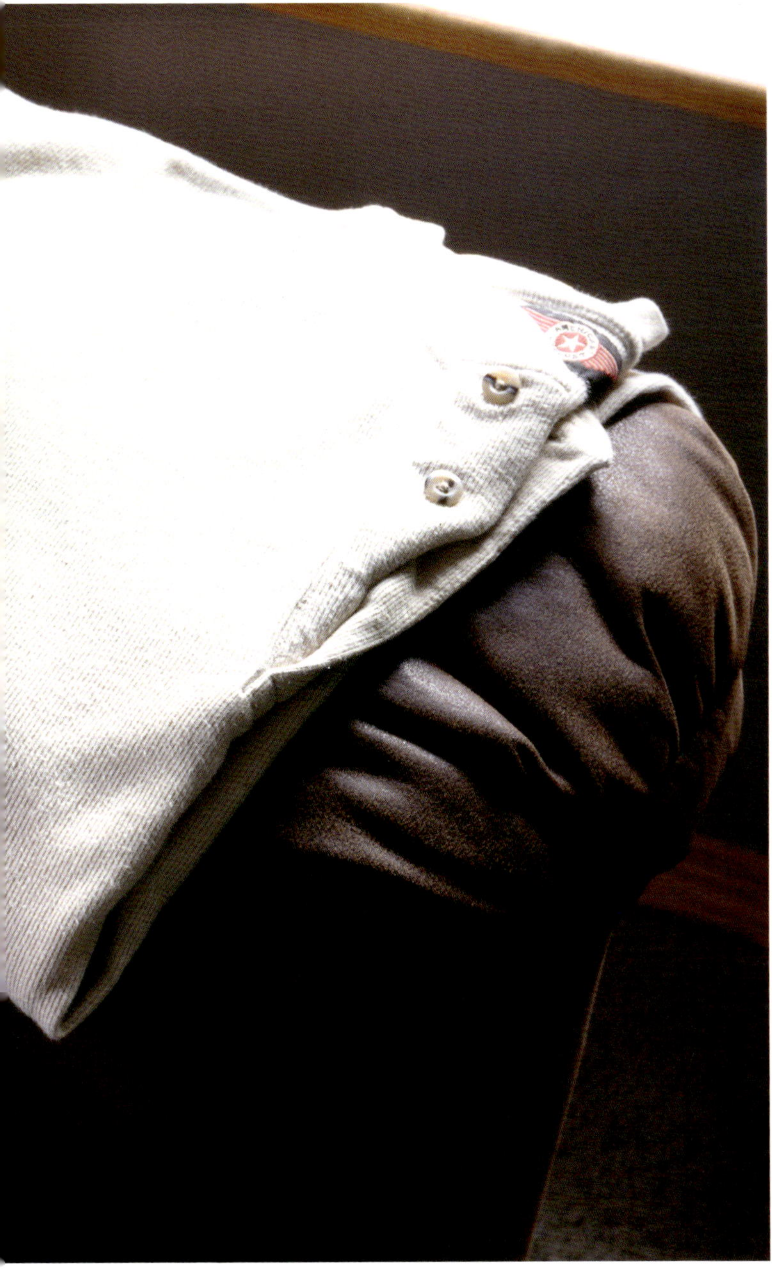

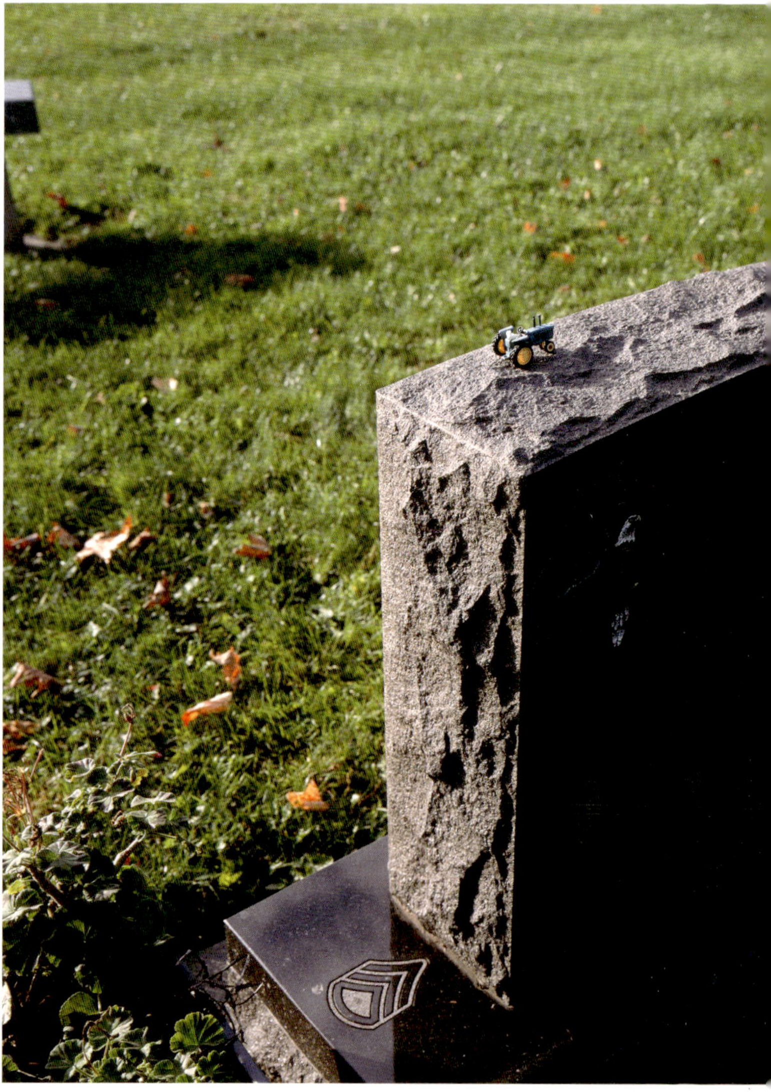

# WHITING*

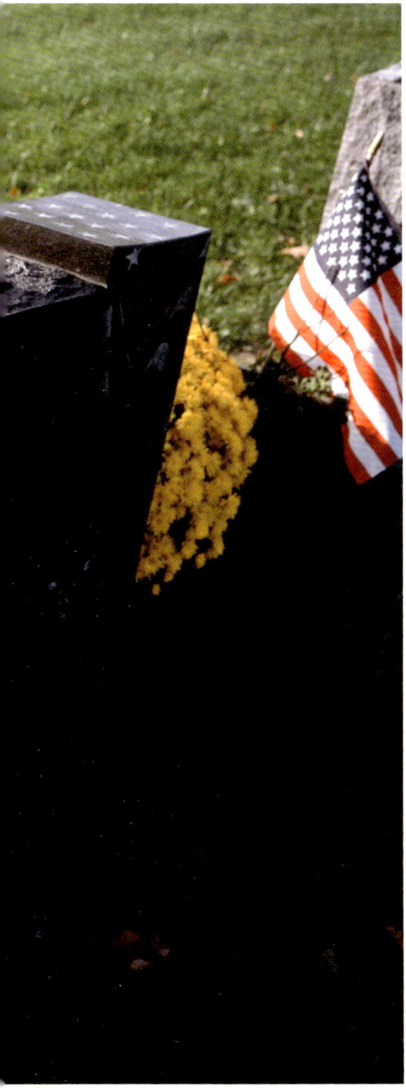

*Father

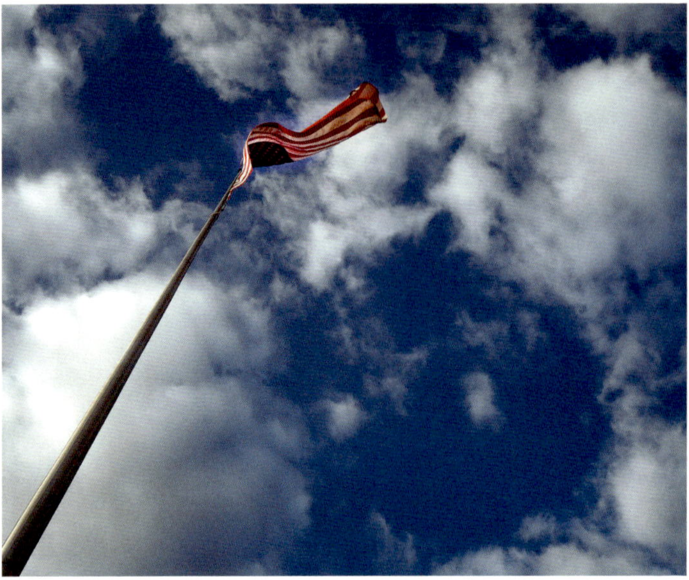

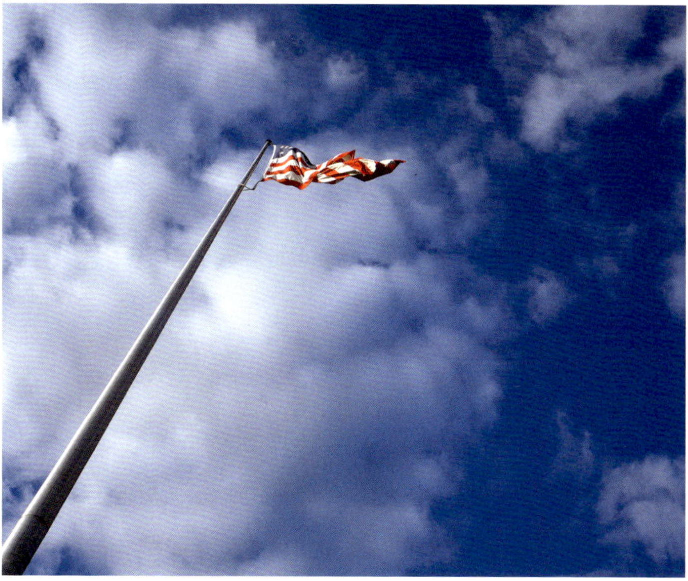

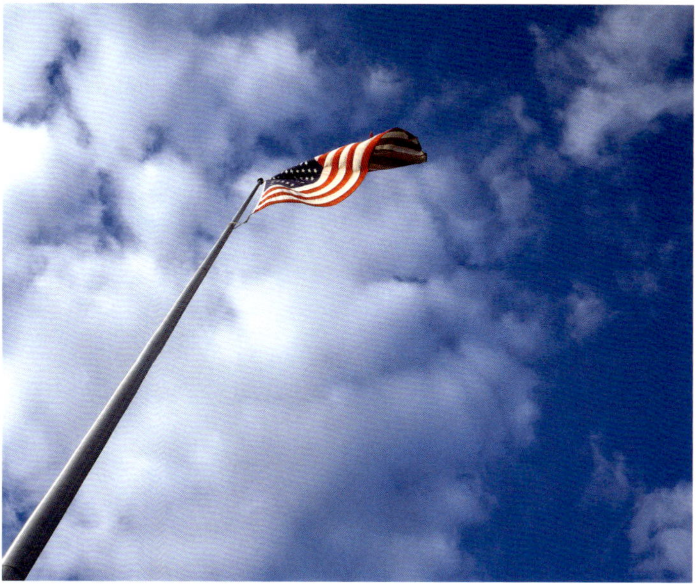

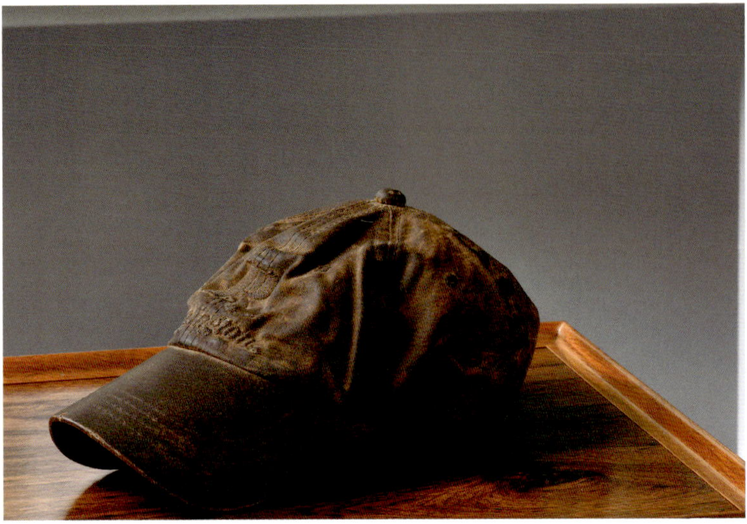

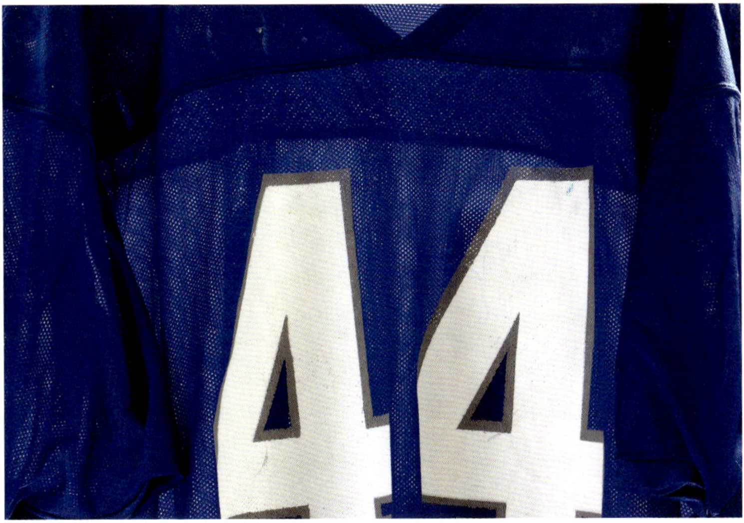
44

# WHITING*

*Mother

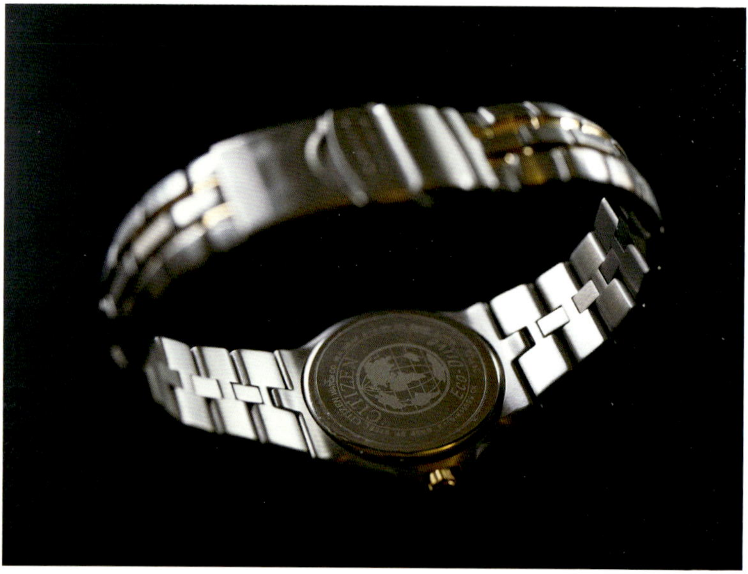
CITIZEN

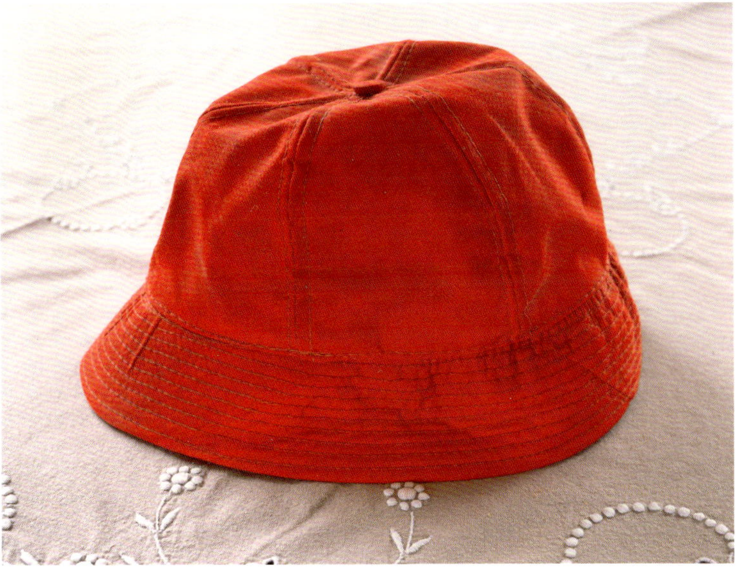

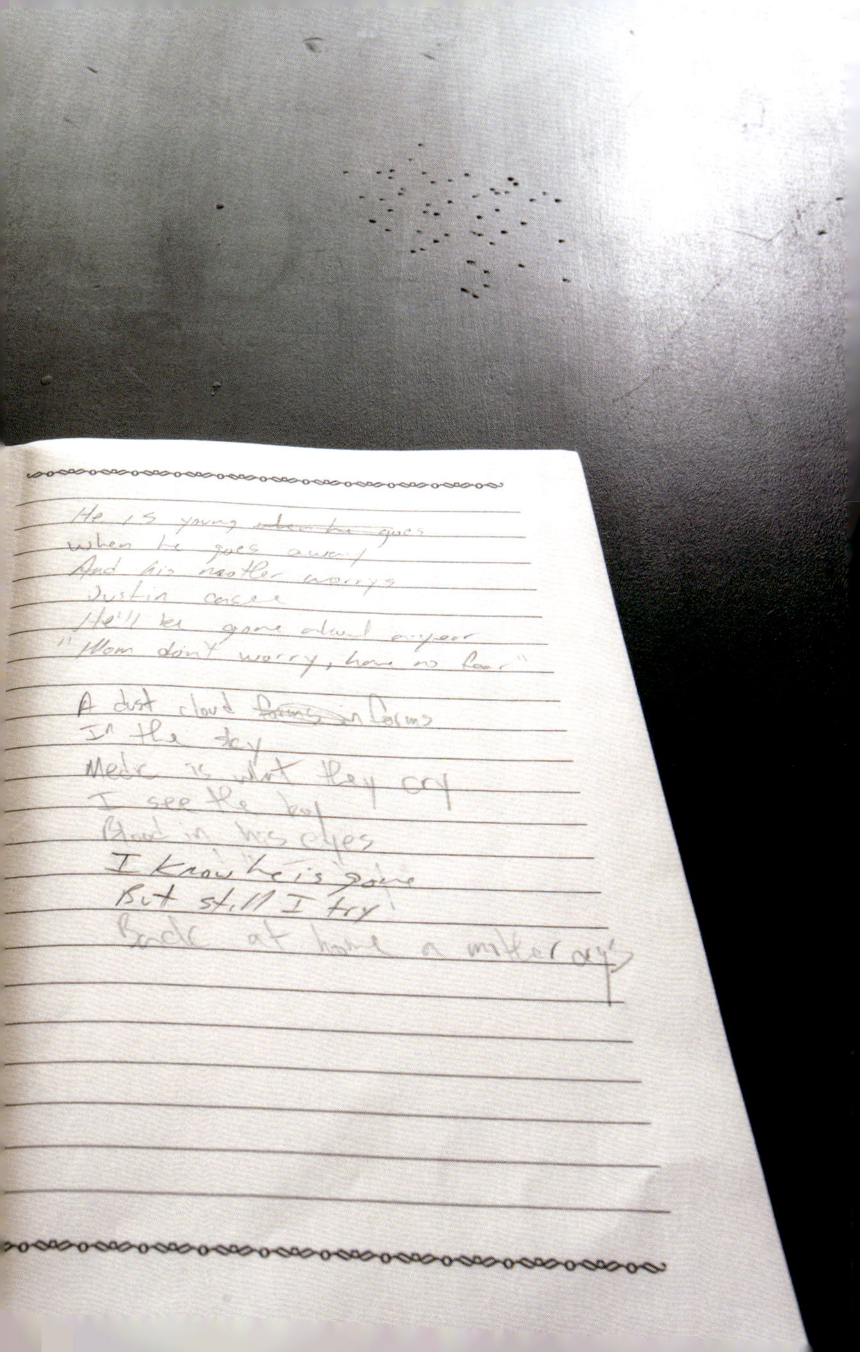
He is young when he goes
when he goes away
And his mother worrys
Justin case
He'll be gone about a year
"Mom don't worry, have no fear"
A dust cloud forms in forms
In the sky
Medic is what they cry
I see the boy
Blood in his eyes
I know he is gone
But still I try
Back at home a mother cry's

N.O.K.

# NEXT OF KIN

Inbal Abergil

Daylight

Cofounders: Taj Forer and Michael Itkoff
Creative Director: Ursula Damm
Copy editor: Elissa Rabellino



ISBN 978-1-942084-35-8

Printed in China.



Daylight Books
E-mail: info@daylightbooks.org
Web: www.daylightbooks.org

*For my mother, Fabian*

# GYSGT JOHN BASILONE, USMC

KILLED IN ACTION FEBRUARY 19, 1945, IWO JIMA, JAPAN.

*From a conversation with Diane Hawkins, niece.*

We lived with my grandfather and my aunt until I was five. So, I still tell people I heard stories about my uncle when I was in my mother's womb. My aunt didn't have children, so she took us on as hers. She had, like, a museum in her house of my uncle's stuff. Her whole life was really built around it; she became like the spokesperson for the family. She said to me, "Diane, one day you have to promise me that you're gonna do something for Uncle Johnny and his memory. You're gonna make a film, a documentary." So I said OK.

Medal of Honor, Navy Cross, Purple Heart, it's heroism—he was the only enlisted marine to receive both the Medal of Honor and the Navy Cross in World War II. They said that he held off 3,000 Japanese troops after his 15-member unit was reduced to two other men. It went across the whole island—they said as soon as my uncle died, everybody on the island just said, "Oooh, Basilone got it, Basilone got it." So, strategically, he brought his men to a place where they got into a better position, so they wanted to give him a second Medal of Honor, but they just don't do that in the military, so he got the Navy Cross. That's another high honor. He was like their protector, and there were different stories—some say a mortar killed him, the mortar came and his guts were out and he was just like sticking his guts back in the stomach and still running.

My grandfather would just talk about how they had the parade for him and they named a ship after him, they named streets after him. There's a Basilone Drive in New Jersey, on the town park; there is one in Santiago. There is a bridge in New Jersey, there is a piazza in Santiago. I mean, you kind of remember this is a little town in New Jersey, and all of a sudden there is a hero. And these are people who just are hardworking people; my grandfather is a tailor. I mean, my uncle was in *Life* magazine when he was still alive, when he was selling war bonds.

When my uncle died, my older cousin said that the newspaper reporters came to my grandmother's house, and they're the ones who told her that he died before she got the letter.

All these letters that women wrote to him and the letters of my uncle.

So this is like one of the typical women letters [*laughs*]: "Hello Johnny, you don't know who I am [*laughs*]. You don't know who I am, you have met so many of us at the continental," something. "I took the pleasure of writing to you as you are the first Marine I ever had the address of, I guess you won't be able to find time to drop me a line." So the funny thing is, they start off wanting to hear from him and then they ride away. That's the way women were then: "Oh, but you won't have the time." Like she says, "I would like to hear from you but I'm sure you won't have the time. I really would like to hear from you." So there she says right after, "If you have any spare pictures of yourself, I would appreciate very much if you would send me one for my album of servicemen. Thank you and I am looking forward to hearing from you."

"Dear John, I want to find out if you were the marine we passed in the car on the highway October 16th the day we came on our way home from our football game, we played—and I'd better get to the point." Well, they're all saying the same thing, silly girls. "I read the article on the *Life* magazine about you and saw your picture in the paper. This afternoon I thought we were just passing some soldiers, but when I looked, well, I noticed John Basilon sitting in the car, it had a New York license plate. He looked like John Basilon, anyway, that made me a little excited because I remember your picture. Maybe you remember me passing in the car and asking, 'Are you John Basilone?' Your two buddies shook their heads yes, so I took it for granted. I would like you to answer this letter and tell me if you ever were the one I saw after all. It's been weighing on my mind. Will you please let me know?" Sincerely, Someone Louise.

I sat on my aunt's bed when I found all these letters. For hours and hours and hours and read through them. So my uncle always ended, seems lots of time, with "Your Loving Son"—I wonder how they keep and not fade, because it's pencil.

He was into the Hall of Fame, they inducted him into the New Jersey Hall of Fame. This was the year with Queen Latifah, Martha Stewart, all of them. The Marine Corps League in Fort Lee, um, fought really hard to get him into the New Jersey Hall of Fame, so they were kind of proud of it. Class of 2011 New Jersey Hall of Fame. And Tony Bennett, Mary Higgins.

Ooh, here is one: "Dear Mrs. Basilone, Frank Sinatra has asked me to reply to your letter, as he is out of the country. Mr. Sinatra is not presently accepting any materials in connection with film, television, et cetera, nor is he any longer in film production. Thank you for your interest and best of luck with your project." So this was my aunt trying to do something with my uncle; that's why she said to maintain [*laughs*], so I'm just saying, her persistence in trying to do something in his memory.

# SSG CHRISTOPHER J. BIRDWELL

KILLED IN ACTION AUGUST 27, 2012, AFGHANISTAN.

*From a conversation with Pam Birdwell, mother.*

We can be buried with Chris. If he was married, then it would be available for his spouse. And we just learned this. We had to determine how deep they were to dig it and then how many places to leave open to be buried with him. Just something you don't think about your own death at that time. Although you would trade yours for his so that he could live a little bit longer and experience things that you've experienced and he would have made a great dad.

Are you familiar with the book *The Giving Tree*, by Shel Silverstein? When he was a baby and very early on, he would lie on his back, we'd lie on our bed, and I would just hold the book up because they see so well in black-and-white, and so he would just kick and get so excited about that book, and that book just seems to correlate with his life. "Well, I wonder if by reading that—" We did that so often, almost every day, and I just wonder if it just stuck with him because it's like the ultimate—you just give everything of yourself. He was very much a boy. Very active and adventurous. He was always a thrill seeker.

This is Chris's favorite ornament. Every year he'd come and say, where's my ornament? And it just cracked him up. I was out one day and we found this ornament of a little boy on skis and he's hit a tree, and that's exactly how Chris broke his leg. He was going so fast—he leaned over and his leg was out and that's what went into the tree and just snapped his bone, so then he had to have these metal bars....And ever since I started decorating this tree, I just haven't taken it down. It's not in our way, and I like having it up to honor Chris, and it just makes me smile when I see it.

That's his uniform. Our casualty assistance officer had it cleaned for us and he had all of the medals updated so that he received all of his, and I just didn't want to put it away and hang it in a closet. I wanted just to keep it out.

Apparently it looks funny on a hanger on a hook. I'm trying to think who might have his cap. I think our niece might have his cap. I could hang that, then, on top, but for now...

I was standing when they told us. It was just—it was a shock, you just—you hear it but you don't really—I mean, I didn't cry; I know that I probably was thinking—probably expecting me to cry but it doesn't feel real, I can't believe this is happening, so I didn't cry.

I tried to reach out to the soldier that was at the back of the vehicle, but I don't think he was in a good place, and I don't think it was a good time for him to share with us or remember because I asked him if Chris had saved his life. If Chris deserves the medal for that, there's no one else here to ask for him other than me. He can't remember, he doesn't—sort of part of that it's too hard or they're just not ready.

When I was there last Sunday, there was a lady there who goes there every Sunday to put flowers on her father's grave. I think if I were closer, I'd probably be there a lot more often, but since we're not, then probably just as well because work keeps us busy. It's so peaceful, you know—you can go and take a blanket or a chair and just sit there or read or whatever. Sing, nobody will know if you sing off-tune. And if you go there and see the graves, it's just huge. It's just amazing how many people are there.

You try so hard not to forget things because you don't want to forget them. It's just hard to remember, when you have four children and you try and remember and you get confused which child was that. Thank goodness for pictures because it's captured, that memory is captured, and you can remember, especially if you can write on that picture what it was about.

# PV2 ISAAC T. CORTES

## KILLED IN ACTION, NOVEMBER 27, 2007, IRAQ

*From a conversation with Emily Toro, mother.*

I remember right before he was going to get deployed. I had this horrible dream. And in the dream he was killed. I saw it. I saw he was in the Humvee. There was some other guy and I saw he died with someone else.... This was, I think, maybe, I don't know, a couple of weeks maybe, or maybe less than that, I can't remember. I used to remember things, but losing Isaac is like... But from that day that I had the dream, I was preparing myself for what was to come because something told me he was going to die. He was not going to come back home. And he would call me every weekend. He was only in Iraq eight weeks. That's it, eight weeks.

I understand that it's costly, but I don't want him as cargo. I want him back in a plane with someone that's going to escort him. When they brought him back, he was brought back in a private plane.

I saw him, because I said, "Chris, I need to see him, I'm not going to spend the rest of my life thinking what he looked like." Because I was touching him. He seemed OK. I know Chris. He puts his hands on the knee to feel his leg because he was afraid. He says, "I just want to make sure that he's all there." He was touching, he says, "OK, his legs are there, everything is there." And that was it.

His one-year anniversary was Thanksgiving. My mom won't cook for Thanksgiving. I think maybe she did it once in the six years Isaac's been gone because she feels that—Isaac loved Thanksgiving. He used to love to come to my mom's to eat. She feels that it's not a Thanksgiving without him, so she doesn't celebrate Thanksgiving.

I always wear this, I never take it—I take it off when I go to bed, and when I leave I always—they're always with me. And then of course the bracelet, I have his bracelet there with his name, that one has his name and his dog tags tattooed on my back. I tattooed his dog tag, and over here I tattooed the Tenth Mountain, the emblem that says Tenth Mountain.

Everything is in there—the only time I go there is I need something. If I can't find it, I leave. It's just that when I go there I cry. It took me a year before I put up anything of Isaac up. And then when I lost my apartment it hurt, because it's like I put him back in a box and back in storage, never to see him again. When I go to the storage, I get overwhelmed because I look at the stuff and I'm like, "Oh God." Or I see a box that says "Isaac's stuff"; I have a lot of "Isaac's stuff" boxes. Even the little things.

See, my ex-husband, for him, Isaac is dead, let him be. And I can't. I have to remember Isaac. I keep the memory alive. Before he died, he said to me, "Mommy, I'm going to be famous. Everybody's going to know me." "Isaac, please, you're so cocky." He said, "You watch." Then you think about it now. He said it then. But him dying, look what I have done. His name is on a post office. He has his street. His name is on a race car. His name is in Chicago. His name is in a wall in California. His name is in the Rayburn Building of Washington, D.C. So, technically, he's everywhere. And the patches that I made for him, people saw them on the Internet. And they order my patches, so he's everywhere. So, not only in Chicago, D.C., North Carolina—I mean, he's everywhere. So, there's a part of Isaac somewhere all over the United States. Yes, thinking then and now, it's like, OK, this is what he meant.

This is his pillow, this one here, see. These are his shirts, so this is his little pillow. It's his two shirts. This is his army shirt and this is his other shirt. I always keep it like this, and that's it. Yes, these are what I got back. The two shirts and the pillow came back, so I kept this. And that's how I sleep with them; I pretend that it's him. It's not him, but I pretend.

# SGT FIRST CLASS KRISTOFFER DOMEIJ

ARMY RANGER, KILLED IN ACTION, OCTOBER 22, 2011, AFGHANISTAN.

*From a conversation with Scoti Domeij, mother.*

I just can't remember at the moment because my brain doesn't remember things since Kristoffer was killed. I have a hard time recalling details.

It was a media explosion because Kristoffer was killed on his 14th deployment; he is the most deployed soldier in American history to be killed in action.

Well, we'd always talk before and after a deployment. Sometimes he called during a deployment. But when he got married, he called his wife, he didn't call Mom, which is fine. So he would call me maybe a few times during the deployment. And now, realizing what they did and how busy they were, I think it was a miracle I got any phone calls at all.

When he was 17, he called me and he wanted me to let him join the army. I said, "No, I won't do that." And then I said, "I would prefer that you go to college." So he says, "I'm tired of people telling me what to do, I'm tired of people telling me to do my homework and clean my room." And in my mind, I'm thinking, "And you want to join the army?" [*Laughs.*] The boy is in for a rude awakening. But mainly he said, he just wanted to jump off airplanes and blow up things; he wanted to be an Army Ranger. After his first deployment, Kristoffer said, "I never expected to go to war," and I'm thinking, "That's why I didn't want you to join—my whole life, we've been at war. How did you miss this, son?" So he called me when he was 17; he wanted to join. I said, "Don't. Here's my preference," but I said, "If at 18 you choose to join, I will support you three thousand percent." But what I didn't tell him is, in my heart, my heart would not support that. But he was an adult and he could make that decision.

You don't want to believe it. You know it's a reality. I could feel my brain rejecting it. And so basically, even if you're not thinking about your child's death, your brain is processing this trauma and it pushes out everything it doesn't need.

Which just so happens to be your memory. [*Chuckles.*] And so that was one of the first questions I asked Gold Star moms: "When do I get my brain back?" They said, "Oh, four or five years." But I have noticed the difference. And it's uncertain. Last month, I started feeling like I'm falling apart; I felt fragile and what's going on? Your body knows. October is coming, his birthday, his death date. And so even if you're not thinking about it, your body doesn't let you forget. So it's a really interesting journey.

I think he was deployed in August and then he was killed October 22. So, here's the bizarre thing, I'm informed on October 21 that my son was killed on October 22. Because it's October 22 in Afghanistan. That was so bizarre, I didn't know what my son's date was—it's so bizarre to be informed of your son's death date the day before.

So I thought, don't tell me where my son is, I will find him. So I got on the Internet, and this was the early 2000s, spent three days on the Internet, went to Afghani and Pakistani sites that were in English. I would just follow links. After three days I emailed him, and I say, "Well, I think you are at this base, I think you are fighting in these mountains." His commander was furious. "How did your mother know this?" He says, "My mother is smart." So probably for the next five or six deployments, I would try to figure out where he was. One time he calls me and he says, "You know, it's 88 degrees, there is sand in my computer," so we get off. He's supposed to be in Afghanistan, I get on the computer. The high in Afghanistan, it's 47 degrees. So I'm thinking, he's just captured a Kurdish airfield. So I would ask questions and I'd figure out things. So the next time I ask, "So how's the weather?" "I can't tell you that." [*Laughs.*] It was national security. All I wanted to know was what country he was in.

Just one thing that I can't show you that's in my bedroom... are some stars are up on his ceiling that he put up there, in grade seven. I look at them every night. Because I know they have his DNA.

# CHAPLAIN (CPT) DALE ALLEN GOETZ

ARMY CHAPLAIN. KILLED IN ACTION AUGUST 30, 2010, AFGHANISTAN.

*From a conversation with Christina Bixby, wife.*

We ended up having it on my 40th birthday because we had to. I thought, it's my birthday, but I'll celebrate him, his life. I buried him on my 40th birthday at Port Logan.

He has boots upstairs, which still have the mud. I'm not getting rid of the mud. They still have the mud from Afghanistan; he was known as the dirty-boots chaplain because he went where they were. "He was the rugged guy who comes to see us and we love him. He's not afraid to come out here and do this, what he needs to do."

I couldn't explain it, I just had this feeling, and I drove up into my driveway and I drove in the garage and it was just this kind of slow-motion weird feeling... I stood in the middle of my living room and that thought crossed my mind, what if? And I lifted up my blinds, I looked out my window, and they were still there. I couldn't see them, really; I just knew there were some people over there. I thought, what if it is? And I turn around and I say, "Dear God, what if?" Then I went to my computer, eager to find an email from him and I got on Yahoo and the first thing I saw was "five killed in Kandahar." It just screamed at me. I thought, maybe he's just hurt. Nobody had called me yet, nobody knocked at my door yet; I just had this feeling. I turned around and I stood in the middle of that same spot in my living room and then King Kong knocked on my door. I stood there and went, what if it's just that, what do I do? And I walked on there and I open the door and there was the blue uniform, the chaplain, in his dress blues and the enlisted in his greens. I didn't know who these men were except that it wasn't a good thing.

I looked at them, and of course they were struggling because they didn't want to tell me this. They had a protocol to follow, and I looked at them, and the first thing I said was, "Is he gone?" They couldn't say a whole lot of things, and I buried my head in that chaplain's suit and I just bawled. I said, "The Lord gives and the Lord takes away, blessed be the name of the Lord." I loved that man; he was a blessing, a gift, and I just was like, that's it, I'm done on this earth. That's what happened.

I kept thinking, how am I going to tell my boys? And so, three o'clock came and they got off school and they walked the four blocks down to our house, and the first one to come in was Landon. I told them that the kids are coming in now, and he looked at me and he looked at all these people and he said it, he's like, "Was daddy killed?" And we've never talked about what would happen. I didn't say anything. I was sitting in my little rocker, my recliner, with these people around, and then he could see in my eyes that I've been crying and whatever. About 30 seconds later, Caleb, who's happy-go-lucky, comes running up the stairs and he's like, "What's going on?" He goes, "Was daddy killed?" And he said the same thing. I called them over to my chair and I said, "Come here, guys," and I had them sit on my lap. I just held them and I said, "Guys, where is the best place to be?" And they said, "Home," and I said, "Where's home?" I said, "Where really is home?" And they said, "Heaven." And I said, "That's where Daddy is." And they just cried and cried and I held them and then it was like, in their little minds, what do you do? How do you react? And they got up and just ran out and did whatever. I had to deal with reality again and all these people and all the planning. That's how they were notified.

I can imagine, but I'm told this was in the vehicle with him. It smelled like smoke. I don't know how it could have survived. This is the one that's hardest. This is my most prized of all of his stuff. The fact that it came off like this, that's his wedding ring. I don't know. It didn't quite look like that. The heat was so intense that it changed. But, anyway, I'm thankful that the soldier took it, because that's my most precious gift that I got back.

# SSG JOSHUA R. HAGER

## ARMY RANGER. KILLED IN ACTION FEBRUARY 22, 2007, IRAQ.

*A conversation with Wendy Hager, stepmother, and Kris Hager, father.*

With memories it never gets better, it gets different. It's never less clear, it's just as clear today as it was the day it happened.

The hardest part about being a Gold Star dad is the sense of aloneness. When I'm with the dads, we all feel better because we don't have to explain anything. There's six in our group. We play golf.

His brother was allowed to be his escort because he was an officer at the Coast Guard—the image of the coffin at the top, holding one side and having my son stand beside him that's pictured.

I still remember, even at that point after seeing Josh in that coffin, I thought to myself, well that's fake. He is on a special mission and he is going to come back and he is going to tell us, I'm sorry I had to do that to you but they had to put me on a special... one always as a parent thinks, your child should not go first.

I taught him how to hunt and fish and hike and he loved being outdoors, he loved fishing. I'd take him climbing; we did all things that fathers and sons are supposed to do.

Everybody in the military has a nickname. He had three. They called him Task Force. Because if you needed to get something done, you only needed one Josh, but that was the same as an entire task force. Honestly, I can't remember what the other two were.

One of the watches we sent to him and his team was this one, and this one is a cooler one. Kris would wear it all the time. We actually put a second ring on it because you don't want to lose it. But that's how it was. That's one of those things you just carry with you. So, we had this watch and we sort of heard a beep and we couldn't figure out where the noise came from. And finally, one night tracked it down that it was his alarm. And when you run the clock back, you realize it was the alarm that went off and woke him up on his last day. I couldn't turn it off, but for two years the battery lasted; we always had the alarm.

I found a very interesting pickup truck. Dodge Company made a pickup truck with a 500 horsepower engine, and it's a 160 miles an hour truck. It was a great truck—I'm at a stoplight and my cell phone rings and I answered the phone and I could see that it was my daughter-in-law and I said, "Hi, how are you doing?" She says, "We've lost him and I can't talk now. I'll talk to you later." I said, "OK." I'm at a stoplight in a 160 miles an hour truck and I'm five miles from home and I clearly remember saying, I probably should park it, but if I do and call Wendy, she won't be able to come and pick me up anyway. She won't be able to drive. I need to drive home safely and not kill someone, so I literally drove five miles home in a pickup that would go 160 miles an hour. I got parked in front of the house and opened the door and walked in the door and collapsed at the stairs. They'd screwed up, the notification teams.

They originally told us that he didn't suffer, he died instantly, which, I think I said that they're just gonna say that. Then we come to find out he didn't, years later from people who didn't know any better but told us. He actually made a radio call and said, "Whatever you do, don't send anybody."

I mean, Josh would literally go at night with a silenced weapon and protect kids playing soccer. To be safe. And they silenced them so that there wouldn't be a fight. There wouldn't be a gun fired that could be heard. I carry a Glock 26. I feel better to have one. No, I feel the responsibility to have one. If something happened like San Bernardino. I mean, if I was at a Christmas party and something weird happened, and I was unable to make a difference, that I'd never live with.

Four years ago, I needed to heal; I needed something to do to get better, and I looked at my—Wendy, and I said, "I really wanna try and play golf again and do it competitively." 'Cause I'm pretty good at it. I found a golf instructor here that would help me who was also a retired military and combat sergeant in Vietnam. And I asked, "Wendy," I said, "do you think I could start learning that?" She goes, "Yes, you probably can." And I learned how to play golf, and I'd keep Josh beside me on the golf course.

His job was to get his boys back. And they all came back. He saved lives. Iraq had a chance to be a better place because he was there, not because we were there but because he was there as a part of we. They threw it all away, but it doesn't diminish what he did and that I'd go somewhere like Orlando to tee it up for the troops, and they'd introduce me, they'd give me a round of applause. NASCAR the racing car—three years ago, four years ago, I got invited to go to Daytona 500. I didn't know what to expect, I mean, I just said, "That's really cool, I get to see all these race cars and all that, that's great." Then they took me to the drivers' meeting—they introduce me and I get a round of applause, all of the drivers are standing up, they're clapping for me. I didn't deserve that. It's for him. I think it is meaningful for them to be able to clap for Josh, and if I don't do it, they'll never get that. That's why I'm willing to tell my story.

# SGT DONNA R. JOHNSON

## 514TH MILITARY POLICE COMPANY. KILLED IN ACTION OCTOBER 1, 2012, AFGHANISTAN.

*From a conversation with Tracy Dice-Johnson, wife.*

I didn't want a relationship because I was getting ready to deploy that November. She was one of those people that I couldn't forget. Anyway, it worked out in the end, and then once we got together, we just never really looked back.

Explosive ordnance disposal in the military. That was then; now I'm National Guard and I'm still an EOD—explosive ordnance disposal. Yeah, which is basically army bomb squad. I was stationed here and I met her on St. Patrick's Day and, uh, we hit it off.

She went ahead and deployed, so—we're both in Iraq the first time. Then because I got extended, I could get an extra vacation. So instead of going to Qatar I would choose to go down to her, she was at Nasiriyah on the south side of Baghdad. So, I went down there and stayed a week with her. We're not allowed to be a couple yet in the military, 'cause "Don't Ask, Don't Tell" was still in effect, so we still have to hide our relationships. Pretty much everybody knew, but that's the thing that "Don't Ask, Don't Tell," if nobody asks you any questions, you don't have to tell anything.

I got this house because when I came back, I knew we needed a place to heal. When I came back, I was messed up and I wanted nothing to do with anybody, especially my family or her family. I wanted nobody around. I wanted a place to heal, and I knew that she needed a quiet place more so than I did. So, I basically got this house for us to heal.

It was 2010; I proposed, but under "Don't Ask, Don't Tell," if you're caught in a marriage, pretty much, you are automatically kicked out of the army. Neither one of us wanted to lose our careers or what we do—I mean, you serve because it's part of your heart, you serve because it's who you are and you want to do something for your community or for your brothers and sisters, so we didn't want to lose that.

So, fast-forward to September of 2011, when "Don't Ask, Don't Tell" was repealed, and we're gonna try to get married on our anniversary of October 10. Then we found out she was up for deployment again for Afghanistan, and so it came down between our scheduling and stuff like that, if we don't make this happen, it's not gonna happen. We got married in 2012. We were not allowed to get married here in North Carolina. So we went to Washington, D.C.... So it was really like a 24-hour elopement [*laughs*]. We just ran up there and done it, but it was kind of our lifestyle. We travel a lot. We were busy a lot. We rode motorcycles a lot. We would love to be on the go, and our favorite place was home. Anyway, she started doing her pre-deployment training like about two weeks later. And "Don't Ask, Don't Tell" had been repealed, but none of the laws had really changed.

Well, I didn't know. I woke up because she hadn't called. She was supposed to call. We had talked on Sunday. She was supposed to give me a call before she left out on patrol, and she's like, I'm gonna get up early and I'll give you a call. I'm like, I don't know who you think you're fooling; you don't get up early for anybody [*laughs*]. So, I'm like, just give me a call when you get back. Because of the time zone difference, I knew that she should have given me a call between 9:00 and 10:30 at the latest. Anyway, I woke up and it was 10:30. I was like, something's not right. So I got on the Internet, and the first page I went to, in red letters, it was like, three US casualties, Khowst, Afghanistan. So I knew that was her unit, and I knew it potentially was her.

I just knew she wasn't coming back from this deployment. It was just one of those things. Because I've been deployed, I know that the first thing that happens is they do a media blackout, communications blackout. They cut off the phones. They cut off the Internet. They cut off everything but necessary military traffic, so they have time to notify family members, so it's not found out over social media or inappropriate means. I started calling around, and I found out that they had been hit.

I called her mom. I was like, "Look, something's wrong with Donna's unit. I don't know what yet." I'm like, "But if anybody calls, you need to answer the phone." I called her sister, told her to be aware. Make sure that somebody was at the house in case somebody came to the house. I knew they weren't going to come here because I knew they weren't going to be allowed to come here. I was pretty much a realist. I hate to say it, but I knew that the military still didn't recognize me as her spouse, even though we were legally married. And I tried to bury my head underneath the pillow and just sleep the day away because I didn't want to face it anymore. Her sister called me, a little bit about an hour later, and told me that the people with uniforms are here in the house and told her that Donna had been killed.

I asked her to have them wait there for me. So, I called a friend of mine and had her come get me 'cause I wasn't in shape to drive. And I grabbed our marriage certificate and went over there, and I told him, like, "Hey, I'm her wife." But they weren't coming here to give me notification. I had to go to track them down and force them to give me a notification. I knew in my heart, I did, but again, I'm her wife. They should've respected me enough to notify me. They weren't gonna let me go up and see her being brought back on American soil. I was not recognized as her spouse whatsoever. I was not recognized as anything to her.

Fortunately, the only reason I was given any information is because her mom passed the information on to me. If it wasn't for her mom treating me as her spouse, then I would've been shut out completely. She allowed me to have a vote on the type of casket, where she needed to be buried; she allowed me to have a voice, and then she took it into consideration and made a decision. Now Donna, rightfully, made her mom the person in charge of disposition of her remains—it is called the "PAD." Which is fine. But it's still not the same as next of kin; I should have been considered her next of kin, and I wasn't considered her next of kin.

So at the time, her will was in Afghanistan with her; that's all kind of important because without her will, I wouldn't have been able to keep our house, and everything would have gone to her parents, her half of everything. Fortunately, we were able to get the will. Going back to bringing her home, fortunately her mom allowed—and I say allowed, I mean, I hope you understand the impact of what I mean by allowed, I mean, 'cause she didn't have to. If we have the relationship we have now, I would not even have been at my own wife's funeral. She allowed me to go to the funeral. She allowed me at least some dignity to the situation, and I was allowed to go and see her body brought back on American soil.

It was in Dover, Delaware. Soldiers who are killed in combat are flown into Dover, and then from there they go to autopsy, and they are prepared for their military funerals from there. Her mom also advocated for me to be her dignified escort, which means you get to escort the fallen soldier to their final resting place. Because I was still military and because of my rank, I was allowed to be her dignified escort back home. Part of the heartache about that was, like even her wedding ring—she did not have her wedding ring on, that she was wearing when she was killed, and this is a necklace I keep it on me at all times. I'd bought her this when she graduated law enforcement. It is St. Michael, which is the patron saint of protectors. These were supposed to be given to her mom because I wasn't considered her next of kin, and it really hurt that I had to give her our wedding ring. I do what I was supposed to do; I turned everything over to her mom, and then her mom turned around and gave it to me. Her mom was such a good person; she is the only reason I probably have any sanity right now.

Her mom allowed it to be put in her obituary that she was survived by her spouse, Tracy. Those are the copies of those medals, because her mom insisted that I be given a copy of all the medals. I know a lot of people who probably will go, well, you got the medals; it isn't the same thing, it's not the same thing. I wasn't presented with my wife's medals; these are copies. This is not the same, I hope you understand.

Obviously I wasn't recognized as her spouse, so I wasn't given widow's compensation. I wasn't recognized by the veterans' affairs—now, that has nothing to do with her life insurance or anything like that, and it has nothing to do with her will. Spouses of fallen military members are given what is called DIC. It's Dependent Identity Compensation—DIC income—and I didn't qualify for that because they didn't recognize me as her spouse, so that was a legal fight, and I took that to the news. I went public with the situation. Honestly, it wasn't necessarily to take care of me by any means, because I am still healthy enough to take care of myself and stuff like that, but I just didn't want it to happen to someone else. Once the legal definition was changed, they can recognize me as her spouse, and finally I was able to get DIC, but more importantly, it was for everybody else.

I'm still in the National Guard, yeah. What really makes it hard, because I do love my country, I really, really do, but there are times it feels like it doesn't love me back, because I only ask them for I think what's fair. I'm not asking for anything above and beyond. I'm just asking for the right thing to be done. Things to be rectified to where it's proper, but I get that life's not fair, it's not.

Things were just on a high for us. We were one of the newer, stronger out and open same-sex couples. We were both stable in the military. We were good role models, and she wanted us to be good role models.

One of the things that she was complaining about when she went on deployment was the good-old-boy network. Good-old-boy network is where guys stick together, and no matter if they are good or not, the guys will stick together because you're just a female and you are not as good, even though you're 10 times better than they are, so it's called the good-old-boy network. "Oh, he's OK, he's a boy, he didn't come here to do this." When he has absolutely no experience or skill set to do it. Now that is very much a reality in the military, but I have not experienced it in my job. Donna experienced it in her job a lot and is probably because of the different jobs we did. When I was in civilian law enforcement, I experienced it.

Then these are memorial tattoos for her. Donna did want a tattoo of our favorite saint before we deployed, and of course time ran short, though she wanted "Missing you much and Loving you more." After she left, I went ahead and got the tattoo of "Missing you much and Loving you more," and then it turns into whenever we were apart, the song that always rang in my head was "Ain't No Sunshine When She's Gone." It's a beautiful song. I did it after she left, so these are memorial tattoos, and this is a full moon over the ocean. Many times we spent time together, it was a full moon over the ocean.

The dogs were our babies. The two boys out there—the two youngest ones—they were her boys. The blue one and the brown one—the gray one and the brown one—they were her babies. Honestly, if it wasn't for the dogs, I would've killed myself. I'm being honest. I knew that I couldn't leave them without having a home. They would've just been separated. Who knows what would've happened. They would've lost their home. They would've lost their world. So honestly, the only reason that I didn't commit suicide was because I loved our dogs. I think they're souls. They are souls that we made a commitment to love and take care of for life, so therefore I honor that.

The biggest thing that I have of ours is just our home. We built the warmth that's here. I mean, it didn't look anything like this, and I think, when we worked on our home together, it was like we were building our symbolic home of love at the same time. This home is a living testament, and for the most part, everything I still do here is just fulfilling what she wanted done to the home. This is where I heal. This is my safe place where, it's weird because it was originally why I got it, right, was for a safe place for her, but it's my safe place now.

We lived that last year—I know the saying goes, like, "Live like you are dying"—we did so much that last year. We were constantly on the go, we were constantly on the bikes, we were constantly at the beach. She was just, like, she was trying to get us as much life in before she knew she was leaving. Kind of made sense. We were the first same-sex couple, who, being legally allowed to be married, had a casualty of war, that could've, should've, been recognized but wasn't.

# SSG FLOYD E. LAKE

## KILLED IN ACTION JANUARY 20, 2007, IRAQ.

*From a conversation with Linda Lake, wife.*

I opened the door, I talked to them, and they said, "Unfortunately, we have to inform you that there was a Blackhawk helicopter and all of the 12 soldiers, your husband was listed on the manifest but we didn't have any DNA to show for sure if it was him." So I said, "Well, when are you going to get the DNA?" She said, "We're going to get back to you." She said, "Yes, based on the Geneva Convention blah blah blah," she said. "It's definitely him, but we need to get his dental records."

They brought him to Dover. They asked me if I wanted to bring him home and I said, "No," because I wanted to bury him in the Virgin Islands. Even though they offered me to bury him at Arlington, he doesn't like cold weather; my problem was I didn't want to bury him there because of the snow. So I wanted to bury him where it's always warm, so he's going to keep warm. People thought that I was crazy, but I said, "No"—this was in January when I buried him. They called me in October of 2007 and said they found more pieces. I was like, "What?" I said, "Where did you all find these pieces?" They said, "On another part of the helicopter." And so each family member had two funerals. So I have two graves. Each one of us has two graves.

When I go to Walter Reed and I see soldiers, I say to myself, "Maybe one of them is my husband; maybe he lost his memory and they don't know he's walking around." So every time I used to go to Walter Reed, I'd be watching people. I'm looking at their name tags to see if anyone is... And then one day I said to myself, "OK, you're going crazy. He's dead." But they didn't find—I said, "They didn't find a body, so how is that possible?" And then I said to myself, "He's dead. I just made up my mind and say he's dead." If he would have come back, he would have been back already. But I just told myself, "He's dead"; I told my kids, "I think your dad's dead." And they were like, "Yes, Mommy. We buried him." And they said, "Why do you think that?" I said, "Because I can't find him; he's not at Walter Reed. I can't find him." My son and my daughter thought I was going crazy but it was just me.

Just like I was telling my daughter, we'd go out and I'd see couples and I said, "I will never grow old with your dad, and that's one thing I'm going to miss a great deal, growing old with him." I said, "That's one thing I'm going to miss the most." I know eventually I have to move on, but I'm still not ready.

"This is your dad's truck." I said, "You will be the best person to take care of it." So everything, how his father left the truck, he doesn't want to change anything. When you open the compartment, his work ID is there. I said, "Andre, why don't you want to take out the work ID and put it up and put it in here?" He said, "No, this is how Dad left his truck and this is how I want it."

This was a Christmas gift from Iraq. That was from one of the gifts. My daughter has a stuffed animal like this. She doesn't go anywhere without it. When she goes to sleep at night, she calls him Camel, Camel has his pillow and his blanket. One time she went away and she told me, she said, "Mommy, can you please cover Camel? That's all I have left of Daddy, please." Right now, it needs to be stitched up and she needs it to get stitched, but she doesn't want anybody touching it.

# LTC JAIMIE E. LEONARD

## INTELLIGENCE OFFICER MARINE. KILLED IN ACTION JUNE 8, 2013, AFGHANISTAN.

*From a conversation with Liz Harman, sister.*

Feeling like I had to finish up all Jaimie's loose ends. We're a blended family. So she was the oldest. So it goes, her, and then I'm 11 months younger. And we are real sisters, blood, with the same parents, and then I have two stepsisters. So our mom died when I was 12, me and Jaimie's mom died when I was 12, and then my dad got remarried, and then the two stepsisters came, and then it was us four, and then they had two kids. So I have a younger sister and brother that is half. Yes, six altogether.

It's like her smile. She had an ear-to-ear smile always. So, definitely one of my favorite things. She loved sunflowers. I have, like, a ton of sunflower stuff of hers.

We always used to joke with her; we were like, "What level of clearance do you have?" She just, like, gets mad at me for asking questions. And then we would just, like, laugh and get that big grin smile. She had pretty high clearance, I tell you that. It was Germany, Bosnia, South Korea, Iraq, and then she got into this special program for the Joint Chiefs of Staff in D.C., at the Pentagon, and then went to Georgetown. That was the only three years she was in the States consistently. We thought she was gonna be president. Like, really thought she would be president one day.

I always ask her, like, "Are you afraid?" She's like, "Would we want somebody on the front lines being afraid?" I'm like, "You got a good point but, like, are you really not afraid, or you're just saying that?" Like, I don't know. She believed in the people, like, the Afghan people. She knew that there were risks, and she was willing to take them.

She had a higher expectation; she was hard as nails and very professional. So, for example, with Trump being elected, I kind of wonder, like, it's her thing. She would never, ever badmouth a president because he is her boss, ultimately. Like, if you're in the military, the president is the boss of all people.

So, she would never, ever say anything negative about any president that we had, so I wonder like how her reaction to this would be, what would be her take on it? So then when my sister died, the two army guys were outside, and then they—everybody had different guys, 'cause we were so far away from each other. And I tried to get rid of them quickly, but they didn't want to go. I was like, "I know, I know," and I'm like, "I just want to go inside," and they're like, "Well, we need to come in." One, we were not expecting anyone, and I was like, "Our house is probably a mess," and I'm like, I just wanted them to go away. And, uh, they didn't want to go away. We didn't have a choice. They—I guess they have to do what they have to do. So it was a chaplain and a major.

Because she was a woman, and because her ranking was so much higher, a lot of the time, she got her own room. You can only bunk with a woman, and you're only supposed to bunk with people of your rank. When she would be deployed, she would bring these things with her. I have a lot of rugs from Afghanistan. So I was like, I'm just gonna use those rugs until we distribute them because I'm not gonna buy a new rug. 'Cause, like, you know, what's the point? I like seeing those things and like remembering where they were in her house. And then that makes me think of, like, memories that we had.

It took a good year and a half to go through all of her stuff. She had so much stuff. And because she was deployed so much, she... like there was all this stuff... she had bills from 50 years ago. She had checkbooks from Arizona, when she was in Arizona with her Arizona address. I am like, "Why have you not thrown these out?" Like, it was just easier when she was packing just to throw everything in the box. We spent, like, a whole winter drinking and going through boxes. Like, it took us a long time, probably like eight months—it's still not done. There's still stuff down there that we need to figure out what to do with it.

That Volvo out there is her car, so then I ended up getting it. She freaking shipped that from Germany; she was really excited about that. She liked to work hard, but then when she wasn't working hard, she wanted to enjoy life, like she'd be in a dress if she wasn't, like, in her army garb. I don't know, it's hard because, like, the car will eventually die, and then what am I supposed to do?

My best friend's mom took a bunch of her uniforms and made me these three teddy bears. So, these are her uniforms that she actually wore. She made these teddy bears, and I get, like, all of them. She has a bunch of different uniforms, so this one had one of her patches from it. So, I love this like it was supposed to be one for me and one for each of my girls, but they're all for me. Major Parker was like, "I don't know if you're gonna be allowed to see the body, blah blah blah." I'm like, "Well, you're gonna have to make that happen because I'm going to, it's either you're gonna allow me or I'm gonna open up the thing myself," like it's not gonna be OK for us not to see her before we bury her, 'cause, like, I'm not gonna believe you that she's in there. So we insisted and we did an open casket at the wake.

Every time she got deployed, we would talk about it, but she was gone so much that it would be like, yeah, yeah, yeah. In the beginning I used to ask questions like, "What do you like, blah blah blah blah, I wanna make sure. She was like, "Liz, it's not gonna happen," and I'm like, "But I need to know," so I always asked her West Point or Arlington, and she said she doesn't care. She said, "Do what's good for you guys, because I'm not gonna be here." So, West Point. It's closer to visit her.

I'm like, "I need a tree or something; I do not like the scenery." So then she said, "Well, I have another spot that I can show you." We walked over, and Paul Hokie's grave was there. [*Silence.*] And I knew she knew him. She knew him and she worked with him when she lived in D.C. for those three years. So when I saw him, I was like, "OK. She can go here." So when I go there, I, like, go to his grave too, and his family does the same.

# CPT JESSE MELTON III, USMC

KILLED IN ACTION SEPTEMBER 9, 2008, AFGHANISTAN.

*From a conversation with Janice Chance, mother.*

I've got a lot of the ribbons and the papers, the commendations, but it was so much stuff, I just put them—the medals and all, his Purple Heart, I kept that in a box, that's in a box, but it wasn't anything I really focused on. I was so concerned about the lives that he touched and not so much all the awards. It's good that he had the awards but they collect dust, and soon they go away and they mean nothing to people when I'm long gone from here, not unless somebody preserves them in the museum. I found out he donated a uniform to the museum down in Parris Island that he wore when he was in Iraq.

I watched those marines take my son's body out with great precision, the way they honored my son. I was very pleased, and they stood guard the whole time by my son's body, paying respect. I went in and they made sure he was OK for me to look at. When I went in, he didn't look like himself. His face was swollen because he had a burn on the side, and they had covered it up with makeup so I couldn't see the burn.

That time I was a Gold Star and a Blue Star. My daughter was still serving currently active duty, and so is Jesse. I had two Blue Stars and then one Blue Star turned to Gold, which was Jesse. Nine months to the day that my son was killed, I was speaking at the Women's Memorial building at Arlington with my son behind me. Only God could have given me the strength to do that.

I salute his picture, and I sit down there and I cry and I say, "Jesse, I really miss you." I miss his hugs because he was a hugger. He would hug me before—that's the last thing I remember, before he went to go to Afghanistan. I didn't go to the airport with him. My husband took him but I was so tired. So he said, "Mum, I love you, give me a hug. Give me a hug." He was always hugging me, and we would talk all the time. Jesse would come to my room when he was growing up in high school; every night we would talk.

I have a big picture of my son that I carry around in my car. When I'm at Arlington, I set it there at my dead son's grave. When I go to Arlington, I go to meet people. I go up on my son's grave, "Jesse, I know you're not there," I say. I'll go there especially Veterans Day, Memorial Day, to see somebody come to the path that I know, that knew him.

That's the one that I pray with; I use that Bible every day. I wrote a little note in it to Jesse when I gave him this Bible. I told him to write in the margin of his Bible when God speaks to him to put the date. If it was something significant, then underline it so you can go back and look at the year and say in 2005 this Scripture spoke to my heart.

I had to get a huge storage unit up here, not too far from my house, and when that truck pulled up, I was there by myself. I started feeling sick. I had to sit down on the ground. Sit down on the ground, I said, "Oh my God, this is all my son's stuff. I can't believe it. Wow." And I just couldn't, I started feeling sick to my stomach, and I said, "Janice, you got to get it together because you've got to go through these things."

One mother said, "How can you smile and have so much joy?" She said, "And your son was just killed?" And I said, "Well, it's because of the divine connection," I said, "I have a relationship with the Lord Jesus Christ," and I said, "My faith is what sustains me." And I said, "I know where Jesse is, and I'm going to see him one day again." Even though my heart breaks, it will never heal, but God has enabled me to move forward in my pain and do good and carry on his legacy of service, because Jesse wouldn't want me to sit around mourning.

I had a dream when Jesse went into the Marine Corps, 1997, 1998—I dreamt that I saw my son lying out on a stretcher. Then there were no wars on the horizon. Not a one. And so, I said, "Why did you guys send him out there?" That was said in my dream and I woke up. I never, ever shared that dream with anybody, not even my son. No one knew that dream until after Jesse was killed. My son called me before he was deployed to Afghanistan and said, "Mum, I had a dream that I'm either going to be wounded or killed, but I'm going anyway." He said, "I want to go change the world and make a difference." I said, "Our time is handed," and said Psalm 31:15, "Our time is in God's hands."

# LTJG ROBERT W. MOINESTER

## HUE DETACHMENT, NAVAL SUPPORT ACTIVITY, DA NANG, UNITED STATES NAVAL FORCES. KILLED IN ACTION JANUARY 31, 1968, VIETNAM.

*From a conversation with Raymond (Ray) Moinester, brother.*

Robert, then Barbara, myself, then my younger brother, John. I remember one of the things—it's the first time he came on leave. His toothbrush was in the holder with everybody's, and so I think it was my sister who said, "All the toothbrushes are home," because he was the first one to leave.

Back then there was a draft. War was going on. He was gonna be drafted. He wanted to fly. So, Robert went in during the Vietnam War as a navy officer, and the short version is, he wanted to go to flight school and he could not land. They put him multi-engines, and he couldn't land a plane with one of the engines cut off. So before they dropped him, he volunteered to drop out of the program and became a supply officer and went over to Vietnam. None of us were drafted. We were all kind of raised to go in the military.

Well, he was the one who explained the birds and bees, so to speak. He actually was more of, like, a father figure. Robert was, he's kind of the glue that kept the family together, he really was.

Again, this is not something I'm proud of, but I was 16, I was playing football. I was in good shape, and he and I got into an argument when he came home on leave, and we started to wrestle. He got on my case, I got on his case, and the next thing you know, we started [*laughs*]—we got into each other, I remember that. I knocked him. I got on top of him, and then I was scared because I actually was able to take him; that one time I was able to take him. He was 5-foot-11, about 185 pounds, in excellent shape.

I'm trying to think. See, I get a little foggy on this. I remember him. I was playing football. I remember he was supposed to leave for the West Coast, and he had got bumped off his flight because something happened. And he ended up coming to my football game. I was playing football in high school.

My birthday is late, so I was actually a 16-year-old senior. So anyway, as I'm playing, I look up and there is this navy officer in the stands. So he got to see me play one last game. He spent the night again, and then he went the next day. I was—just shook his hand and good luck, that type of thing.

I was home that day. I was home with my mother because I was going to go to work in the afternoon. A letter came from one of his men expressing condolences because this guy figured we must have been notified by now. But ironically, that's the first thing we heard. Well, panic struck. I picked up my father at work. There's then the two navy officers came that day. My mother, she—I mean, she started screaming. Bear with me, because that—that's a very—I remember, that's a tough day to remember. I'm—I'm good. I'm OK with this. There were so many people killed, and I don't even know how long it took them to get his remains. It was almost the middle of February. We found out that he was killed on January 31. I remember my father saying, "You know, the world still goes around." He says that we're getting off for a while. I remember him saying that: the world goes around, but we're getting off for a while.

Louie Pasutto was the first person killed in our neighborhood, and it was a shock to everybody. And I remember this young man. He was about my sister's age. He was in the army; he was killed by a sniper. There was a marine after; then my brother was killed. And then right down the block: There was Robert Lodge, and he's, to this day, missing in action, presumed dead. He was an air force pilot, shot down. My buddy Richie, when the lottery came out, my number was number 56. I would have been taken anyway. Richie was the first, number one.

We used to follow it because it was the first war on TV. When he was killed, that really came—that hit me. You're watching the news and stuff; you say, this is for real. Oh my God. It really hit me. After all that hurt and after we buried him, it really hit me that I want to think this through here, and I know I couldn't—I couldn't join the Marines right then. And I couldn't do that to my parents. And I remember not following the war on TV anymore.

My mother, her life revolved around the ship. She christened that ship, and therefore she had VIP status in the navy. They reweaved the bottle that my mother smashed on the ship and—so Barbara got that. Once in a while, I've worn a tie clasp. But I'd be afraid to lose it. The cufflinks, I have. My brother John got his medals. My nephew Chris got the duplicate. There were duplicate medals made, so he got the duplicate in a case. The pilot got his sword. These are, like, highlights. There's so many other things, and we still have so much stuff down there. I just wanted to make sure people got what they felt they wanted.

Robert was 24. I was 18, so John was 16. Uh, I'm so sorry, 15.

# LTJG ROBERT W. MOINESTER

HUE DETACHMENT, NAVAL SUPPORT ACTIVITY, DA NANG, UNITED STATES NAVAL FORCES. KILLED IN ACTION JANUARY 31, 1968, VIETNAM.

*From a conversation with Barbara Moinester, sister.*

I think to a great extent, some consolation for my parents was the naming of the ship *Moinester*, which was an incredible honor when you think about it. A young JG gets a navy ship named after him for his heroism? Unbelievable! It started off as a DE—destroyer escort—named after my brother, a young JG killed at the age of 24.

He was 18, I was 14, so there's a big difference age-wise. But some of his friends would want to take me out, and of course my father would never have allowed that. But because I was gonna be with my brother, it was OK. He used to love to dance. And sometimes we'd go out, and our dates weren't the best dancers. We'd dance with ourselves the whole night. We would just dance.

At the time, there was a lot of conflict over the Vietnam War. And there was a time that Robert actually thought that he didn't agree with the war. And he thought he would go to Canada. And there were heated arguments because my dad, as a World War II vet, that's not acceptable. I don't know whether my brother really believed in that or [*laughs*] he wanted to get my father to argue the other side of the point. But the bottom line was, after he graduated from college, he went into OCS. He volunteered.

It's funny, it was like yesterday—it was 43 years ago, you kind of go back and forth. It was horrible. I can still see myself; I was sitting in the phone booth, no less. My dad said, "I—" he tried to say this, but "Robert's been killed." I think your whole life freezes in that moment [*sobbing*]. You were kind of in a strange place because you got word that he had been killed, but his body wouldn't come back for another two weeks.

While he was overseas, he had left his car. He loved his car. It was a 1965 Le Mans convertible. My parents had the car, and they gave me his car to go back and forth to college until the casket came back. So I had his car, which I knew how special it was, and he taught me how to do stick because he had four on the floor—it was a convertible, was a neat car. A really neat car. In a way it was like, "OK, I still have him because I have the car," and that was symbolic more than anything else.

My parents got very involved in the ship. It was a living legacy. So my mother was the sponsor of the ship when it was christened in the Avondale Shipyard down in the New Orleans area. When the ship would come into the Brooklyn Navy Yard or up to Maine, they were always there. They were very involved. And I think that was their way of saying, we're assisting in keeping the legacy of Robert alive by being involved. So, of course, Uncle Robert was a concept. My boys, they had never met him, but having the ship was, "Wow, this is really neat." You know how little boys would look at things like that.

A lot of the memorabilia had to do with the ship. So, for some reason I said, "I've always liked the ship's bell." OK, fine, you get the ship's bell. But then my parents had my brother's original medals. And it was all encased. There's only one of them. So, who gets that? So, Ray and I kinda put our heads together and said, "I think John should have the medals. Let's ask him." Then Raymond said, "How about this—do you want it? If you don't want it, I'll keep it." My son, Bryan, wound up with Robert's Bible, and he was honored to get Robert's sword. Bryan's daughters being adults themselves, they should have their own tradition. They should have their own artifacts.

This is as clear as the day he said it: "Barbara, when you graduate from college and I am out of the service, we've got to live in San Diego. It's just a fabulous town. It's a wonderful place, it's young and vibrant." He went through some training in San Diego. And I remember him saying, "Well, that's a plan," and you know, after he died, I got a teaching job there. I fulfilled our promise to each other.

# HN WILLIAM F. ORTEGA

## MARINE EXPEDITIONARY FORCE. KILLED IN ACTION JUNE 18, 2010, AFGHANISTAN.

*From a conversation with William Ortega (father), Maria Ortega (mother), and Edna Ortega (sister).**

*Conversation was held in Spanish, which Edna Ortega translated into English for the author.

We are five sisters and him. He was born in Nicaragua. We came here when he was three years old. He left to deployment when he was in the process of becoming a citizen, so when he left, it was still in process. When he was killed, they told us that he became a citizen.

He enlisted with the navy, but in California he started working with the Marines as a medic. And supposedly I hear that when they have respect for a person, they start calling him Doc. So he instantly got that name really quickly... He was a navy and he also became marine force. He had the right to be able to wear marine uniform and navy uniform. So, he was basically both, and he got happy about that 'cause he's like, I'm able to rock the Marines and the navy [*laughs*], and we're like, yeah.

On his last visit at home, the time that he was here, he would just, like, start bear-hugging everybody; he'd grab you and squeeze you—wouldn't wanna let us go. When he woke up, he'd just be hugging, and so he went to sleep he'd hug everybody back. [*Laughter.*] And that happened every single day, and then my mom was like, "What is wrong?" He's like, "Mom, just let me feel you. Let me hug you—that's it."

Before he left the house, he told my parents, "Just know that if I have to give my life for a fellow marine, I'm gonna do it..." Those were the last words that he told my parents. And I remember my dad told him, he's like, "Don't go trying to be a hero, because heroes always die." Then he was like, "Wow, you know if I had to give my life for a fellow marine, I'm gonna do it, because he's my brother." And those were his last words.

My mom had come back from a restaurant with my dad, and there was a black car... They'd see it drive, the car then stops, and then drive back, but then go back; they were, like, indecisive of where they are going. My mom told my dad,

"Something is wrong," and my dad is like, "Don't worry, that's nothing. Come inside, come inside." And then she's like, "No way, I have to see the car leave for me to go inside the house." And then they were waiting outside, and they saw them stop at one of our neighbors' house. And two people came out; they were dressed in the uniforms. At that moment, they talked to the neighbor; she had a son that was trying to enlist. So then when my dad saw that, he told her, "Don't worry, they are probably trying to look for her son." She's like, "I have to see the car leave." And then she saw they went back in the car, and then they drove. They were, like, about to leave, and my mom's like, "OK, they are leaving in a minute." But then they stopped; like as soon as they turned in the corner, they stopped and did a U-turn, and then they came back and they parked in front of our house. When they got off, they approached her and my dad. She said instantly she knew, because my brother spent a year preparing her. He was like, "Mom, if this ever happens, don't ask any questions; just know that I'm gone. 'Cause when they arrive, it's never good news."

On Father's Day is when we received his body. So, he received—we received my brother's body on Father's Day. My dad says that he felt torn apart, that he felt that he was devastated like he basically couldn't feel anything anymore. Basically, all his feelings and emotions were pulled out of him and thrown in the garbage. Father's Day has no significance for him anymore. Why celebrate Father's Day if—what's the point? Like he doesn't see any point in Father's Day anymore.

William was the last one to be brought out, and that's when we saw that it was three marines on one side and three navy on the other side; both of them had brought him down from the plane.

It was in a zip-locked bag, and we saw her take it out, and then she started taking the things out of the zip-locked bag; she would, like, put them on the table, and then we recognized it 'cause there was my brother's wallet, things that he carried, and then it was his watch, his pens. She just lined it all up, and when she was taking it all out, like, you could see dirt fall from it. His wallet wasn't black anymore; it was, like, brown 'cause it was full of dirt. This is what was on him, when they found him. And he had a picture of them in the wallet. He had a Bible and a little notepad and stuff like that.

The phone calls when he would call, he would talk to both of them. It would always have to be Mom first. We would get jealous 'cause we are like, "Why you always gotta go first?" She'd give him advice or they'd talk about the Bible, like she'd tell him, "Oh, read this verse. Read that." And then he was like, "OK, Mom, we'll put Dad on." And then when my dad got the phone, all she heard was, "Ha ha ha ha, oh my God ha ha," like, all laughing. My dad said that when they would talk on the phone, he'd tell him stories about him going out to the bars or to the club: "Dad, you're not gonna believe it, but when I go out, it's like I'm a girl magnet. Like all the girls get attached to me. They always want to talk to me, and I'm like, 'Chill, chill,'" and then my dad's like, "Wow, don't let that opportunity slide. Use protection, 'cause I don't need no random kids... We only have one life—live it. Live it to the fullest." My mom said that she never knew what they talked about till right now: "Oh, no wonder they laughed so much." [*Laughter.*]

Till this day, we really don't know what happened, though, because of all the versions that they told us. So, our casualty officer had told my parents to go to the base because there was somebody that wanted to talk to them. It was another medic's father. And his son got home, so I guess he told his father the story. He was on speaker, and he only spoke English, so I would be translating to them. "Oh, my son, you know, he's very, like, devastated of what happened, and right now he was, like, not in the right state of mind to be talking to you guys, but he told me what happened with your son." And the story he gave us was that they were on an actual battlefield, and my brother was aiding a wounded marine. He said that they screamed to him—they were like, "Doc, RPG" and, like, they had told him ahead of time for him to move because they said that my brother looked back, and when he saw it coming, he didn't move. Like, he had the opportunity to move but he didn't move. He just, like, covered the marine he was aiding. The casualty officer, she basically, like, cut the phone, cut the conversation when he started getting into details. She cut the call and said, "OK, well, gotta go, we gotta go. I'll make sure that they have your number," and she didn't give it to us. That's when my parents start thinking, like, well maybe that was the true story, because why else would she cut that off and then not let us have, like, a deeper conversation with him?

This is a letter that her and my dad made 'cause they wanted to read it in the ceremony, but they didn't give them the opportunity to read it out loud, so my mom kept it, though.

My dad says, when he gets ready for work every morning, he comes through the living room; he just looks around, and when he goes here, he's like, "Hi, good morning... I'm gonna see you later, but not right now, not yet, won't join you today." 'Cause he knows that see you later are not going to be too soon. But it's gonna be sooner than later.

He says he don't like going to that area in the living room, because when he looks at his medals, he starts thinking, "What did you become to me? Pure medals... Where are you?" He's like, "This is all I have of you, like you're just medals right now. You're just medals." He says, "I told you to not try to be a hero because the heroes end up in the cemetery. Like it's just full of heroes in the cemetery." That's why he doesn't like this room, so he just comes through it.

# SGT KYLE B. OSBORN

## SNIPER. KILLED IN ACTION SEPTEMBER 13, 2012, AFGHANISTAN.

*From a conversation with Maggie Osborn, wife.*

I lived in a townhouse in Italy. At 11:00 at night, I didn't know who was buzzing my gate. But I kind of had that sickening feeling. I didn't immediately let them in, because I didn't know who it was, so I walked out there. I saw the glint of the buttons on the uniform from the notification officer. And as a military spouse, you're taught that if someone shows up at your door in just the "cammies," then they came home, they just reentered. If they show up in dress uniform, it means they're gone. So I knew exactly what it meant when I saw them. I let them in. We walked down to my house. They asked me if I wanted to sit down and I said, "No, just tell me. I already know what you're going to say, just say it." And they proceed to do the, "On behalf of the president of the United States of America, we're not happy to inform you..." At some point, my friends put me to bed. I remember getting woken up the next morning and being taken onto the base to get a new ID card that no longer said "active duty." It said "active duty deceased" on it.

The day after is when my friends packed a suitcase for me, and I got put on a plane and sent back to America.

It's rare, but they granted access to escort him from Dover to Indiana. So I got to be a part of the escort team. And it was basically a little puddle-jumper plane with the pilots, me, and then a military escort from the unit in Italy that flew with me. And then Kyle was in behind us in the little cargo area; it was a tiny little plane. And we flew from Dover to Indiana. The first time I saw him was at the funeral home.

That's when the personal possessions are given to the representative who's escorting the service member back home. Since I was there, they handed them directly to me at that time. And I got his dog tags and his wedding ring and a picture that he had in his pocket at the time. And then his cap card (which is his ID card), with a hole punched through it. They punched a hole through the little computer chip that's in it, so that it can't be used again.

Kyle wanted a closed casket. His reasoning behind that was that he didn't want the last image of anyone to have of him be of his dead body. He wanted the happy images that we're always going to have—the laughing, the smiling—not him in a casket. Unfortunately, also in his last request was he wanted to be buried with his wedding ring on. Dover didn't do that; I had the choice to either let the funeral director put his ring back on or I could do it myself. And I decided that even though he didn't want me to see him, that since I was the one who put the wedding ring on the first time, I should be the one to put it on the last time too. So that's what I did, and I had to see his body; it was—it sucked [*chuckles*]. My first reaction unfortunately is that I laughed. Just because of the way they do them up, put makeup on him. It looked like him but it wasn't. They want to make them look as normal as possible, even if no one is going to see him—it's just what they do for everyone in Dover. But yes, so I just had a moment with him and I put his ring on. Unfortunately, they couldn't get his gloves off because they'd dressed him in full dress blues, which was the first time I'd seen him in dress blues because he refused to buy them. That was his big stake against the army: not buying a new dress uniform. And he finally got one. But they had gloves on him, and unfortunately we couldn't get them off. And I had to put his ring over the glove. And then I had them close the casket completely. That's it. I'm done.

He had a pair of cowboy boots that he and his best friend had gone and gotten together, and I really don't see the point in keeping cowboy boots. So I gave them to his best friend, and he used them as a placeholder at his wedding for the best-man spot that would have been Kyle's. The one thing that I'd be heartbroken about would be losing the pictures. The pictures are everything I have, our entire life that we had together. Which is why, thankfully, the week before he was killed I went and got that external hard drive, and had everything saved on it.

He loved the army. He loved it. Obviously, he loved it enough that he was willing to give his life for it. That's what he did.

# PFC STEPHEN WILLIAM PICKETT

KILLED IN ACTION DECEMBER 14, 1967, VIETNAM.

From a conversation with Victoria Miano, sister.

The only picture that we have of him from over there is that one Polaroid that he sent, and he had Instamatics, but as he said, he had them sent to the developer but we didn't get them back. I don't know how they send them to the developer—I don't even know where do you send pictures in Vietnam to get developed? I don't know.

I had gone on the computer, I think, about, maybe, 1998, '99, so I went on military websites where you could post on boards and stuff like that, a lot of people looking for other people, and I didn't hear until—it must have been a couple of years later. Somebody had finally answered. They sent me an email, and all the email subject said was, "Your brother," and back then it was you never opened email from people that you didn't know. So I did open it, and it turned out to be his sergeant in Vietnam. We went back and forth a couple of times because he didn't want to give me any information, if I was really a family member. Finally, I had just the one Polaroid of him when he had gone into the tunnels and he had pulled out of there a North Vietnamese flag, and I scanned the picture and I sent it back to him and he said, "That's definitely him."

Then he wrote me a two-page email. I read it. I was just sobbing because he explained detail by detail what happened that morning. You could feel the emotions coming out from him, and he explained it with such detail, as if he was talking about what he had for breakfast that morning. So vivid was the memory of him.

It wasn't a day that was, like, celebrated. They didn't celebrate my grandmother's birthday anymore; he was killed on her birthday. It was around Christmas; I mean, we had his wake, and the funeral was just a couple of days before Christmas—I think we buried him on December 23. I think it took about a week in between that time, so Christmas was just like—Christmas just went. It was for years and years. I don't even think until I was in my 20s, until I was in my own place, and then it was like, "Oh, we can celebrate Christmas again. It can be a happy time. It doesn't have to be a really depressing time."

I think it was just realizing now we didn't talk about it. It wasn't something you were proud of. You didn't walk around going, "My brother was killed in Vietnam." It was almost like your brother was a baby killer and stuff like that. Because people hated the Vietnam War. Not everybody, but that was pretty much the essence of it.

I don't know. I've always felt like Stephen has always been like my angel watching over me, and I just wanted his presence around. To keep his memory alive.

It was one of those accordion-type openings up of a turkey decoration because Thanksgiving was coming up. So I sent him stuff, I even sent him—even in the letter as I read it, I sent him a puzzle. I don't know what I was thinking. I guess they got a kick out of it—what are we doing with a puzzle in the jungle?

He was vice president of the class of 1965. He was in Sodality, Guard of Honor, athletic council, cross-country-runner track. He was in drama, debate team. He was on the Owl, which was—that's the yearbook. Dance committee. Cheerleaders. I don't remember that. And intramurals. So this was the year that he graduated.

This was the newspaper article. It was on December 19, 1967. He actually was a paperboy, so this was the newspaper that he used to deliver. He used to deliver the paper.

Actually, that's one of my greatest blessings is to have his letters. Usually at the Vietnam Veterans Recognition Day I read his letters. And that's always just been great, just to keep his memory alive. It means a lot.

# SSG STEVEN R. TUDOR

KILLED IN ACTION APRIL 21, 2007, IRAQ.

*From a conversation with Kendra L. Lynn, sister.*

He gave this doorbell to me when I first bought this house, and I never put it up until two years ago, and he had this made for us. When we got this new door, my husband finally put it up two years ago. I love when I walk in, I would see this and I would think of him every time someone knocks on the door. Yes, it's him.

Our whole life, all we had was each other, and they don't talk about it. And it's one of those things like I don't want to bring up. It's not like we don't know it's that day, the day he died or his birthday is coming up. Next month is his birthday. We don't forget those days, but it's one of those things like I don't want to add to their pain by calling them up and be like—usually, what happens is we just shoot a text and just be like, "Love you. Love you."

As bad as it sounds, I never worried about him over there. Like I just thought that, after my sister died, I thought, statistically, this can't happen again. You know what I mean? Like, "He's fine, this can't happen again." How could this happen again? For it to even happen once is horrible—statistically in my head, it can't happen again—and then four years later almost to the day, she died April 16, and he died April 21. I hate April. April is the worst month ever. And it happens. So I don't take anything, any of that for granted, and you never know.

It was just always us, and Steven was just finally so happy and he was married and he had two kids and they'd just bought a house and—it's like he got robbed. I mean, that's how we feel, like he got robbed of this, his life, out of all people.

When you get this stuff back from Iraq, they wash everything, they delete his computer, nothing could be on it—which was really hard because—pictures. So he and I and my other brother, he took us to Florida. I want all of those pictures and they're just gone. They get rid of everything. Everything's cleaned; they wiped the computer out, they go through all of his stuff, everything's washed, like all of his personal stuff. They wash it before—his wedding ring. Everything's completely washed, everything. So there's no scent of him or nothing.

That's something that has been replayed in my mind probably five million times. When you hear the story, you put it in your mind and you're like, "OK, well, I picture him doing this," and then you just sit there and wonder, did he suffer? Did he know he was going to die? Like, what were his last thoughts? The officer that did the eulogy, he said that once it hit him, there was no pain, there was nothing, he was just done. He didn't suffer. I don't know; it's like out of a war movie. You just picture him slumped over in the helicopter and someone's holding him and trying to stop the bleeding or whatever. Then they give him something to make him comfortable and then he passed on the way. I guess we'll never know. Because, that's the hardest part for me. I want to know that he's OK. It bothers me, how scared he must've been if he knew that he was going to die. That's one of the hardest parts, just not knowing. I don't know. I don't know if I'll ever know, I won't.

It's been seven years ago. But it's still right there, and it doesn't seem like seven years. It seems like yesterday; I remember every single part of it, and here every day—there's never been a single day that I've not thought about it and, like, his dog tags hang in my car. His picture's on my desk and everywhere. There is not a single day that he's not in my thoughts.

My goal is to actually go to Iraq and mark the spot where he died. That's one of the things I talk about to the kids—when you die in war, it's not like when someone's murdered here, like there is an investigation, and they usually find the person. No one will ever find the person that did this to my brother.

# SSG JUSTIN R. WHITING

## SPECIAL FORCES MEDICAL SERGEANT. KILLED IN ACTION JANUARY 19, 2008, IRAQ.

*From a conversation with Cynthia Whiting, stepmother, and Randall (Randy) Whiting, father.*

Before they get deployed, they have, like, a sheet of paper they fill out; it's almost like a last request or a will in a sense—where do you want to be buried, what kind of service you want? So, you had a little guideline of what they would like you to do. Justin didn't want any sad songs.

He wasn't shy about telling anybody exactly how he felt. He knew exactly what leached out in all times. In both ways. If you do good, he would be the first one to come over and shake your hand.

He joked about when he went to basic training, 'cause he worked so hard at the farm, he said, "This is easier than being on the farm." "This is easy, and they're feeding me three times a day."

He fell off the wagon backwards over the wagon, broke his femur. And he lay in there on the ground, but you see it. He looked like he had two. He never cried, and he was five years old. He said, "Well, Dad, it looks like I broke my leg."

It was gonna be Nathan's first deployment. Justin already had two. So, we pulled up out here, and there's a van across the street, parked. When I drive by, I was in the passenger seat, and I looked and I see there was a chaplain. And you know right away. We didn't know which child. Could've been any of 'em, really. When we got out of the vehicle, he said, "Mr. Whiting." And probably three quarters expected it to be Nathan. It was his first tour and... maybe did something stupid. So when they told us it was Justin, it really, really floored us. We just couldn't picture that happening. "N— not Justin. No. He's too savvy. He wouldn't let that happen."

Yeah, that was a hard. I mean, as hard as it was, the notification and going through the funeral and everything. Six weeks later, we got a call from the assistant officer at West Point. He wanted to come see us. So he comes up and he tells us, "We have more remains." And he didn't have any details on how, or why we have more remains, but we have more remains. And I don't know if they ever did tell us; maybe when they dismantled the Humvee that he was in, they found pieces. We don't really have the details; we didn't really ask. We may not want to hear the answer, but... when we found out about this, it was really raw. It was like pulling a scab off a wound or something. It was really hard. For the second notification, we had him cremated, and we just did a small service.

"Want a beer?" [*Laughs.*] Because that's what he would say. The first thing he would do is come in the house and he would go right in the fridge and grab a beer and, let's start the conversation this way.

I don't know that we were ready for too many details. As a matter of fact, we had to put a request for the accident report and... when it came, it sat on our coffee table for months, and then I moved it up. I think we are getting closer, don't you? We've talked about it more openly lately than we have.

Here's his football jersey. They actually retired his number over at the high school. That was nice. This was his hat; he wore this hat everywhere. It's all beat up, hole in the leather; he had that always on his head.

He would like to come home for deer season—that's in November. He would try to work out into his schedule; he loves the hunt. This is his first deer that he caught when he was, like, I think he was 15. All this whiteness in the deer—it's called a piebald. It's like a mutated version of a white—they're not supposed to have all that white on them, but it did, so we skinned it, because we didn't want to get it tanned; we misunderstood what we were supposed to do. So it had deteriorated a little bit, and that's why some of the hair fell out in these areas. He took that area and he painted it with the etchings. It came out pretty nice. It should be all brown. First deer, yeah.

They asked if there was anything they could do for us, so we asked Randy's mother, and she said she'd like to have a lock of his hair. I guess it's an old tradition that's kind of gone by, because they had said that they hadn't heard anybody ask for that. Nobody does it anymore. Well, they gave us enough so that we gave some to Estelline and we kept some and then we gave some to his mother. We made a frame. We put his picture in it and then a lock of his hair on the other side. My grandmother was the redhead, and that's where the red hair came from.

# SSG JUSTIN R. WHITING

## SPECIAL FORCES MEDICAL SERGEANT. KILLED IN ACTION JANUARY 19, 2008, IRAQ.

*From a conversation with Estelline Miller, mother.*

My story is just as powerful as everyone else's that I have met. It's very humbling. At the time when they all went in, it was a little unusual to have all the kids in the army. But as the war went on, it became not that unusual to have multiple kids. Amanda always knew growing up she wanted to be a soldier—that was just what she wanted to do. Justin said he couldn't very well have a sister in the army and not him; that would not be very good. He had always wanted to go in, too. Nathan graduated in 2001 and wasn't quite sure what he was going to do with his life. He preferred to ski every day, but that didn't really—it wasn't very profitable. And then 9/11 happened and he basically said, "I can't have my brother and sister in and not me." That's why he went in. A lot of people say they give their kids luggage for high school graduation. I gave mine an army recruiter.

Justin was a Green Beret. Special Forces. They do a lot of things that we may not necessarily know about or want to know about. He deployed twice with his team. Special Forces are made up of 12-man teams, and he was the medic on his team. When he knew that he was going to deploy, he kind of withdrew himself because he had to get in the mind-set of what he was going to be doing and had to focus on the mission. He might call a couple of weeks before they left, and then that would be it. I wouldn't hear from him until he got back.

I think it didn't have to be anything specific with Justin. He could have a good time just sitting around the kitchen table. You could really have fun with Justin no matter what. One of his teammates said at his funeral that he would never—when you were with Justin, you were in good company. And that's true.

The weekend before they deployed, this last time, when Justin died, Amanda and I had gone to Fort Campbell to be with them the weekend before they left. We had such a good time, and it was like my kids being little again. They would fuss and they laughed and joked. I've never laughed so hard just because they're such funny people, and they have such a unique sense of humor. Justin played the guitar. They were just brother and sister fooling around. But it was quite a memory, just to sit there that night and listen to them. But it's like God gives you those special moments to have. I do think he probably had some sense that something was going to happen. When we left that weekend—and remember, his house kind of sat up on a slope—and so as we pulled out of his driveway, he was standing outside to wave goodbye. I said to Amanda, "Stop, let me hug him one more time." I ran up his driveway and he's laughing. I said to him, "Be careful." I said, "You take care of Nathan." And I said the same thing to Nathan, "Nathan, take care of Justin." But he just looked at me with these serious blue eyes, and he said, "Mom, it will be all right." I thought, "What does that mean? Why did he say that?" I remember getting in the car with Amanda saying, "He said it will be all right." No, not like, I will be all right or we'll be all right, don't worry. But it will be all right.

Nathan and Justin were deployed together when he died. They had never deployed together. That was the first time. Justin's team was just north of Mosul, and Nathan and his team were just south of Mosul, that area of Iraq. But that morning, the morning that Justin died, the two teams had come together for some reason, I don't know exactly why that happened. But Justin and Nathan sat that morning. And Nathan says he sat and laughed and joked. Nathan said they talked about who was the last one to talk to Mom or Dad, who would send what, you know. But they had seen each other that morning. Nathan says that Justin got up to leave—he and his team got up to leave—and he said, "Mom, I was able to look in his eyes." And they shook hands, and Nathan or Justin—do you do that with your kids, call them all the same name?

And within a half hour of leaving Nathan that morning, he was killed.

It was Nathan's commander that came and told him that it was Justin. Nathan's the youngest, but he is a grown man. But I think all of us, after it happened, aged a hundred years.

I came back in the house, and within just a few minutes, my doorbell rang. I opened it and I knew. I could tell that one was a chaplain. I saw his cross on his uniform, and the other man had such a baby face. He looked so young. I was a little taken aback by how young he looked. I stood inside the door and the young man said, "Are you Estelline Miller?" And I guess I just looked at him, because he asked me again. I think I was thinking that if I didn't let them in, then they couldn't tell me. But the chaplain said to me, "Ms. Miller, you need to let us in." They came in, and I remember thinking, "This can't be happening because they've always told me—" my kids have always said, and Amanda has deployed, "We will be fine. Don't worry." I had just chosen to live a very naïve life. They said nothing would happen, and that's what I chose to believe. Of course I worried about them, but I never once let myself think something would happen. They came in here and they kept saying to me, "Ms. Miller, we need you to sit down." I kept screaming at them, "Which one of my boys is dead?" And the young man, he stood over me, and I finally sat down, and I'm still never sure why—how that seems to help anyone. Why do I need to sit down? But he stood over me, trying to read this piece of paper, and his hands were shaking. You can see the paper shaking in his hands. That's when he said Justin's name.

Nathan said, "The moment after the captain told me, the first thing I thought of was, I have to bring him home." I think that was just so overwhelming for him, just that responsibility of bringing your brother home.

Hancock, New York. All the family members are buried there. It's just a small county cemetery with a little white church, and my kids went to Sunday school there, and had all the community Christmas pageants in that little church. That's where he's buried.

He wasn't someone that took a lot of things with him because he had to carry it wherever he went. I know he didn't have a lot. It was mostly his clothing. He had with him, for whatever reason, he had a watch that I had given him several years before for Christmas. It was a dress watch. And why he had that in Iraq I have no idea. I had given him a kind of a hardbound notebook. I think the date in it is 2002 because he liked to write things down. It was really more kind of thoughts that he would write down. I gave him this, nothing fancy, just a black hardbound old notebook. And he had that with him. And that was 10 years old—well, six years. I'd given it to him six years before. Why did he have that? I don't know. Justin never wanted me to send him anything because it was too much to carry with him because they weren't stationary. He said, "Everything you send me, I have to put somewhere on me," on his body. He said, "Don't send me anything unless I can eat it."

In some respects, the anniversary of his death is just the marking of time for me. His birthday is, I guess, where I sense the most loss. The most what would have been, what could have been.

The other thing I've realized, over the last couple of years, I think I've kind of figured out why I needed to know all the details of how he died. I wanted to know, why were they on that road? Why was he the driver, because typically he wouldn't be the driver. I wanted to know how big was the explosion. Give me the dimensions. I wanted to know what the Humvee looked like after the explosion. I wanted to know exactly the time that it took from the time the explosion happened to the time they got there, the team got to him. I wanted to know, what was he doing in the truck, was he—or in the Humvee? Were they just driving? Was he talking? Was he singing? Because he was always singing. I needed a picture of what his last moments were like. And again, I think that's why the birthday bothers me, because I knew what it was like when he got here. I needed, I guess, to kind of put the finality on what was he doing when he died. Does that make sense?

Did I tell you he had gotten out of the army? He had done his first enlistment. He had been to Iraq twice and various other places, and he said, "Mom, I'm going to get out." He had kind of had enough of the politics and what was going on over there. He said, "I'm going to get out. I'm going to hunt and fish until the money runs out." He was only out for just a few months, and his team told him that they were headed back to Iraq. He basically said, "I don't want them to go without me."

I think this means the most to me. It comes from someone in Justin's command. I'll just read you the part that touched me. This is sympathy, and then he says, "It was my decision to place Justin's Special Forces operational detachment to the forward operating base at—"... I just thought, what an honorable man that he felt the need to say, "It was my decision." I thought, he must feel awful. And I don't know what that must be like for him. All these soldiers coming back are living with all kinds of issues, whether it's the death they saw or, in this man's case, just saying that I put him there.

"The detachment returned to the closest American base with Justin to ensure he was treated with the utmost respect and honor. Justin was always accompanied by the members of the Special Forces group." And that too meant a lot. That he was never left alone, that Fifth group was always with him. I didn't think that would matter; you don't know. That has meant a lot, knowing that it was that team that stayed with him.

# AN ELUSIVE PEACE

by Fred Ritchin

In the United States we are living through an extraordinary moment, a "post-truth" era of "alternative facts" in which one can choose what one wants to believe. As a result, even history is up for grabs, and with it our notions of heroism and sacrifice.

A leading politician and war hero, John McCain, can be disparaged for having been captured and tortured by the enemy in Vietnam, called a "loser" by the president. John Kerry, another former soldier who served valiantly in the same war, could be "Swiftboated" for his service and, partly as a result, lose the 2004 presidential election. Previously, George H. W. Bush, another war hero, lost the presidential nomination in 1980 to an actor who only played a war hero, Ronald Reagan. And in this past election the Gold Star family of Humayun Khan, killed in Iraq, was also aggressively attacked, their son's sacrifice belittled.

What counts for valor? What does service mean in a society without a draft, where so few serve in the military (less than 0.5 percent, compared with more than 12 percent during World War II)? The concept of service becomes distanced, at times even cinematic, with heroes who can be conjured up and myths that may conceal the more complex, difficult realities that soldiers, and their families, must face.

And in the press, the battles are often shown as spectacles, offering little understanding of what is at stake and little context for the violence. It can be difficult to ascertain the reasons for a war in the swirl of politics; it is often much more riveting, if not productive, to concentrate on the fighting with its vivid explosions and destructive violence. As a result, the individuality of the combatants and of the civilians caught in the crossfire tends to be obscured, and the reasons for the fighting are largely left unexplored.

War photography, which began in the middle of the 19th century, was initially constrained to portraiture and to depicting the aftermath of battles. Small, portable cameras and more light-sensitive films were introduced in the 20th century and were employed in the 1930s by photographers such as Robert Capa and Gerda Taro to give a visceral sense of the conflict during the Spanish Civil War that preceded World War II. These photographers' black-and-white images were published in the large-circulation picture magazines, such as *Life* in the United States and *Vu* in France.

In recent decades, a large number of photographers have depicted conflicts throughout the world, primarily in color. But there have also been a number of photographers who have chosen, rather than adding to the imagery of battle, to explore the often-difficult lives of the soldiers as they come home. Nina Berman's work with severely wounded veterans, *Purple Hearts: Back from Iraq*; Eugene Richards's *War Is Personal*; Suzanne Opton's *Soldier/Many Wars*; Jennifer Karady's monthlong pictorial restagings in the United States of traumatic events that soldiers had experienced in Iraq and Afghanistan; and Monica Haller's Veterans Book Project, containing 50 books featuring the photographs and words of veterans, their families, and civilians, beginning with her college friend Riley ("I want you to see what this war did to Riley")—all of these add to an understanding of what it was that happened, and happens, to people during war.

One can see this work as emblematic of a "photography of peace"—a quieter attempt to understand and even remedy some of the effects of war on those involved, rather than a vivid focus on the fighting itself. This approach may prioritize the well-being of the individuals affected, as well as their families, rather than prioritizing the larger spectacle of war. And in doing so, it can more effectively make the human consequences of war explicit, including to those policy makers who will next be deciding whether to militarily intervene.

Inbal Abergil, herself a former soldier in the Israeli Air Force, was intrigued to investigate the military culture in the United States, and particularly how families cope with loss. In Israel, where military service is compulsory for most, the assumption of potential catastrophe is widespread. In an interview, the well-known Israeli novelist David Grossman cited "an international TV program [that] once interviewed a young Israeli couple and asked how many children they wanted to have. The beautiful bride said immediately: 'Three.' And the interviewer asked: 'Why three?' And she said with a smile: 'So that if one of them is killed in a war or in terror we shall still have two left.'" In 2006, Grossman himself lost a son during the fighting in Lebanon.

Abergil's photographs attempt to make visible the outline of profound loss as it assumes permanence in the daily lives of families. She shows the flagpole upon which a father raises and lowers the American flag every day in memory of his son, buried nearby; the dolls made out of a uniform that sit on a couch in memory of a child; the array of memorabilia that fills a living room; the handwritten letters sent home; a newspaper clipping; *Life* magazine; cardboard boxes filled with stuff; the colorful tattoos covering two forearms reading, "Ain't No Sunshine When She's Gone"; and a "black hardbound old notebook" that had originally been a gift. Similarly to the writer Tim O'Brien's exploration of soldiers' belongings, *The Things They Carried*, during the Vietnam War, these artifacts help us to better understand the soldiers who have been lost, as well as their families who survive them.

Military cemeteries are the signifiers that detail the quantities of loss. Here, in *Next of Kin*, what Abergil is looking at in both her photographs and extensive interviews is a more widespread and personalized geography of grief and of the necessity of carrying on. The battlefield is displaced, and years and decades later the war continues to reverberate within people's homes even as the news cycle has moved on.

And in doing so, Abergil circumvents a "post-truth" world of "alternative facts." By quietly exploring the authenticity and intimacy of mourning, she respects the privacy of her subjects while serving as an indirect conduit for their experience. She does not show the faces of the family members she meets, but finds space via their objects and words to express a memory of what was lost, and a sense of the enormous void that has displaced what should have been.

This book makes it clear that, once endured, war never ends, and quietly pleads that if there is ever an alternative, peace is the far better choice. It also makes the argument that war is much more than a temporary display of violence; seeing it only as such obscures what actually happens, and continues to happen.

As the New Jersey doctor and poet William Carlos Williams wrote in "Asphodel, That Greeny Flower": "It is difficult to get the news from poems yet men die miserably every day for lack of what is found there." *Next of Kin* resembles a poem that has been inscribed in tragedy and hope, in love and memory, limning perseverance, because there is no other choice, decades beyond the battlefield.

Or perhaps it was better said by Pam Birdwell, the mother of SSG Christopher J. Birdwell, who was killed in Afghanistan in 2012: "You try so hard not to forget things because you don't want to forget them. It's just hard to remember, when you have four children and you try and remember and you get confused which child was that. Thank goodness for pictures because it's captured, that memory is captured and you can remember, especially if you can write on that picture what it was about."

This is what *Next of Kin* tries to do as well.

# THE MEMORY OF THINGS

by Carol Becker

*All sorrows can be borne if you put them into a story or tell a story about them.*

—Isak Dinesen[1]

Inbal Abergil's photographic project *N.O.K. Next of Kin* goes to the heart of our humanness. It tells a story about the enormous love we can have for family members, the impossible task of reconciling that love within ourselves when its recipients are taken from us, and the ways in which we are able to conjure their memory through the things they leave behind.

Inbal Abergil focuses on how families cope with the loss of a loved one who has died in war. It begins with her efforts to locate Gold Star families—families that have lost sons, daughters, husbands, brothers, and partners in Iraq, Afghanistan, and Vietnam; during Operation Enduring Freedom; and in World War II. She then encourages these families to tell her their stories, focusing on the exact moment when they were informed of their loss. Time compresses at such occurrences, and grief-stricken people often recognize that their lives have been irrevocably transformed. With a combination of written text and image, Abergil is able to capture this initial shock and its aftermath.

When designated messengers—"casualty notification officers," chaplains known by the cross on their jackets, army officers wearing "dress blues," or enlisted men in green fatigues—walk up a military family's driveway and ring the doorbell, the family usually knows that these people have come to tell mothers, partners, and wives that their sons, husbands, and daughters have died. The mother whose three children were serving in Iraq at the same time surely understood that the men approaching her home were about to tell her that one of her children had been killed; she just didn't know which one. In the military, there are protocols for everything, and, therefore, there is a prescribed way to announce a death. Each bearer of such news must follow the same script closely. It begins: "On behalf of the President of the United States of America..." But even when the person being addressed begs to be told more quickly, the statement nonetheless must be read in its entirety. For the listener, seconds become eternity.

Abergil wants to understand which belongings left behind are most treasured. She photographs them and attempts to capture their singular importance to the families. Easily recognizable and often mundane, these possessions catapult the speakers back to a time when their loved ones were still alive and intact: a pile of photographs, a stack of letters, a pair of old shoes, a cap, a dress watch, brass buttons sealed in plastic, a notebook open to a page of writing, a holiday ornament with the name "Chris" attached, a child-sized stuffed camel from Afghanistan, two shirts compressed together to form a torso and to function as a pillow, a pressed military uniform on a hanger, a wedding ring... These objects stand in for the person who was once alive and for the body that, in some instances, could never be returned for burial because it had been blown to bits.

Abergil photographs these objects directly and without artifice. The meaning of these images rests in the space between the irretrievable past, the pain-filled present, and a future comforted by the memories embedded in each possession. The simplicity of the objects stands in juxtaposition to the magnitude of the loss they signify.

Abergil's documentation of these objects conjures the way in which time can be embodied and made eternal by our response to memorabilia. Not unlike Proust's "madeleine," whose taste allows him to recall lost time in great detail, the visual, tactile object can hold a person's aura, affirming that there was once normality and a shared family life.

In his much-acclaimed 1990 novel *The Things They Carried*, set during the Vietnam War, author Tim O'Brien describes the objects, "largely determined by necessity," that soldiers packed in their rucksacks: "Can openers, pocket knives, heat tabs, wristwatches, dog tags, mosquito repellent...salt tablets...lighters, matches, sewing kits."[2] When soldiers went into the mountains, they added "mosquito netting, machetes, tarps, and extra bug juice."[3] Soldiers also carried more personal objects: letters from girlfriends, good luck charms, the New Testament, M&Ms, and brandy. In addition, O'Brien writes, "they all carried ghosts" and other emotional baggage with them—deep sorrows but also joy.[4] All such things weighed them down while grounding them to the earth.

In *N.O.K.*, we encounter these objects returned, transported back to the United States after the body that had trekked through the landscape with them has been obliterated. Once photographed, these objects recall what is left behind and what can immortalize lost ones to their families. They also represent the weight that passes on to survivors. For a wife it is her husband's boots that retain the greatest meaning. Most important to her is the dried mud from Afghanistan left on the soles. It represents something from her husband's past reality that always will remain unknown to her. Such objects exist out of time, re-creating a fixed past that can never be transformed.

But time also is an inexplicably fluid construct, capable of suspending reality. The slights of childhood—the words used to reprimand us when we are very young—can upset us anew decades later, as if just spoken. Yet something that occurred this morning can be quickly repressed or forgotten. By presenting each object in isolation, Abergil has turned the photograph into a small shrine, a site of remembrance that captures the preciousness of each object. She has found a form within which to contain the aura that these objects radiate for those who cherish them. They come to represent time encased in grief and reflect the process necessary for the memory of loss to recede. That a representation of objects saved by families, accompanied by narrative, is able to conjure such resonant meaning is a tribute to the artist's commitment to convey the power and uniqueness of the act of mourning.

We are reminded that the conventional wisdom—"Time heals all wounds"—is not always apropos. Some wounds never heal. They fade from our immediate consciousness, somewhat, but only after we reconfigure who we are and how we see the world in relationship to them. Negotiating loss, decades later, can continue to require great emotional effort.

In his essay "Mourning and Melancholia," Freud notes that mourning is hard "work."[5] It requires diligence to undo one's multiple and overdetermined attachments to a person. This process of detaching happens bit by bit, as one separates oneself from images, memories, and the ways in which one's psyche has been enriched by someone's presence and now is impoverished by his or her absence.

In his essay, Freud attempts an analogy between mourning and melancholia but recognizes that the relationship between these two states of consciousness is tenuous. "In mourning," he writes, "it is the world which has become poor and empty; in melancholia it is the ego itself."[6] Yet in each there is an abyss that becomes a dreaded obstacle for the grieving person who must negotiate this incalculable space every day as he or she attempts to live life as before.

When someone receives tragic, or even extremely positive but unexpected, news, the deliverer often suggests that the recipient should "perhaps sit down." The concern is that, when receiving information too enormous for the psyche to immediately organize, the body might go into shock. No longer able to hold oneself upright, the person could collapse.

Anyone who has been told something unexpected and impossibly painful knows that one's legs can literally buckle right out from under. One might not be able to stand upright when the will to defy gravity, which is perhaps the life force itself, becomes suspended. In extreme instances, blood even stops flowing to the brain, and the person leaves consciousness temporarily or faints and, at times, even hits the floor.

Inherent in these saved objects—and in the artist's gesture to enshrine and contextualize them through photography—is the understanding that the process of mourning, of experiencing the death of those closest, is ongoing and can take a lifetime to complete. Possessions can define a life, but when they are separated from the owner, who can never return to reclaim them, they can also define a death—both for the soldiers lost and for those who loved them most.

## NOTES

1. Isak Dinesen, interview by Bent Mohn, *New York Times Book Review*, November 3, 1957.

2. Tim O' Brien, *The Things They Carried* (New York: Mariner Books, 2009), 2.

3. Ibid., 8.

4. Ibid., 9.

5. Sigmund Freud, "Mourning and Melancholia," in *The Standard Edition of the Complete Psychological Works of Sigmund Freud: On the History of the Psycho-Analytic Movement, Papers on Metapsychology and Other Works*, vol. 14, 1914–1916, trans. James Strachey (London: Hogarth, 1957), 246.

6. Ibid.

# ODE TO FRIENDS

by Maurice Emerson Decaul

One summer morning, many years ago, I was awakened by a knock at my barracks-room door. I got up, slipped on shower shoes, walked the short distance between my bunk and that brown metal door, opened it, and found the sergeant of the guard, waiting with a pronounced expression of concern displacing his usual fresh-faced grin.

This was a time between wars and we were all so very young then; I might have just turned 21, an old man to that world.

The Gulf War had long ended and September 11 was some months off; that summer morning, I was still invincible, as were the other marines. If you would have asked us about war, we would have answered in the most martial tones that we were the pointy tip of America's very sharp spear and that we were ready to live up to the Marine Corps' reputation. Some of us believed that rhetoric more than others. I believed, though with a growing familiarity with death, the myth of invincibility was wearing away.

In 1999, while preparing for our Mediterranean deployment, a boy in Third Battalion Sixth Marines had made the grave error of standing while mortars were being fired into an impact area nearby, and a piece of shrapnel found him. A safety stand-down was called, and training was suspended temporarily while his death was investigated. None of us knew any details, so we speculated as to why that young man had stood up during the call for fire; was he made nervous by the impacting mortars? Was he scared that the rounds would be walked into his position in error? How had these marines ended up in an impact area? Who was at fault? The answers don't really matter anymore. As a matter of training and doctrine, one might apply lessons learned to educate marines about how to accurately call for fire, for instance; but all these years after, I am left wondering about the family from which this boy came; how have they mourned him? How have they remembered him?

One summer morning two years later, I answered a knock at my door and found the sergeant of the guard. He asked me to follow him to a room shared by two new privates first class. These marines were brand new to the unit, having arrived only a few days before. I had yet to learn their names.

We entered their room, and I moved to the boy lying on his back on the ground. I looked into his eyes. They were brown, as was his sweat-covered skin. His breathing was slow and soft. I tried talking with him but he had turned mute. A corpsman arrived and began to administer care. I looked at the boy and he looked at me. He was still alive behind his eyes. We encouraged him to hold on. We begged him to stay alive. I looked into his eyes and he into mine. The corpsman breathed into him and pressed on his chest. The rest of us stood waiting to do our part if called upon. A clear liquid drained from his ears. I kept looking into his eyes, trying to communicate. I looked into them one last time and watched them go dark.

The corpsman continued his ruthless campaign, trying to force life back into the boy's body. I retreated outside.

The morning and the day would still go on: marines would still need to be roused from sleep, formation and physical training were moments away; the business of the Marine Corps would still have to be conducted. In that moment, I was unaware of how deeply seeing this boy die would later affect me.

A few days after that, his parents flew up from Texas and we eulogized their boy. The language barrier made it hard to communicate, but sympathy was offered, as was a folded American flag. We never did see them again. As with the boy killed by shrapnel, I am left wondering about this boy's parents; how have they mourned him? How have they remembered him?

Inbal Abergil's *Next of Kin* begins to offer an answer. The photos and accompanying narratives offer the viewer an unprecedented and intimate portrait of the homes and lives of Gold Star families. The U.S. Army describes the term "Gold Star family" as being "a modern reference that comes from the Service Flag. These flags/banners were first flown by families during World War I. The flag included a blue star for every immediate family member serving in the armed forces of the United States, during any period of war or hostilities in which the armed forces of the United States were engaged. If that loved one died, the blue star was replaced by a gold star. This allowed members of the community to know the price that the family had paid in the cause of freedom."

The objects photographed for this collection offer a glimpse into the way some Gold Star families memorialize their loved ones, but they also do much more. The objects photographed are highly personal. Some are unique, and many are exceptionally common; a uniform pressed and hung as if it is there waiting for its owner to wear it, a box of hand-carved wooden toy cars, stuffed animals, letters, newspaper clippings, photographs, a Marine Officer sword, boxes in a storage container, a snowboard, a made bed, a shelf with multiple folded American flags. Search your own home—you might find the same objects, and therein lies the empathetic potential of Abergil's *Next of Kin*. In much the same way that we find these objects in our own home, we could also find ourselves next of kin. For a country engaged in a series of long wars, wars in which a minority shoulder the burden associated with war, wars in which casualty counts have been greatly reduced in relation to older wars, wars in which casualties are nearly invisible to the average American, it becomes even more important to humanize every casualty. Abergil's *Next of Kin* does just that.

# STILL LIFE

by Stephen Mayes

Inert, settled in place, and cozy in their domestic settings, the objects documented in the photographs of Inbal Abergil would scarcely register in the eye of a visitor to countless American homes except maybe as a near-subliminal reassurance of normalcy and everyday cultural connectedness. But to anyone opening these pages, the objects confront us with a tightly measured tumult, silently shouting to us about the utmost violence that wrought death in distant lands on the closest kin. The contradictions exposed with such eloquence in these most turbulent of still lives are both an intellectual and an emotional expression of the conflicts and confusions that roil in the lives of those who have survived. For while they depict intimate glimpses of the dead, they more truly speak of the pain of the living. Here is death, and still life.

The many meanings of each object to the surviving partners, parents, and siblings are gently inferred in the accompanying texts that speak of past experience, unfulfilled opportunity, and current shock that something so vital as the heart can be pulled still beating from one's body, leaving the survivor alive without life. And yet life continues.

For us as viewers, the contradictions are different but no less confusing. Anyone motivated to open this book is already looking for a connection, maybe in an intimate search for the meaning of a personal loss, or for comfort found in shared experience, or merely trying to understand the human cost behind the headlines. We are disinterested yet fascinated by these details of lives of which we know nothing but which we understand so fully.

Immediately there's a curious twist in the appreciation of a book that is intrinsically about memory. Photographic images are easily understood as documents of memory because that's been their place in culture for over a century, and we all have some small but significant objects that represent a continuity connecting us with a lost person.

place, or time. The format is familiar, and we move easily into a wistful reverie that seems appropriate to the subject, until we consider that nothing in this book is a memory to anyone but the bereaved, about whom we know very little and whose experiences we can only speculate about. The book in your hands as you read these words is a current experience. Beyond the known fact that soldiers have fallen in conflict, everything we see between these covers is news to us, and we have no experience to account for the memories we now hold as we close the covers and lay the book aside. Of course, we all share the human need for contact, and most readers of this book have a general empathy with those who have lost loved ones. Since birth, we've lived with novels, films, TV, and other media that offer vicarious opportunities to share the lives of others. For the people who opened their inner places and shared these intimate details, there may be a hope that sharing the pain might lighten their emotional load, and public recognition will validate suffering that otherwise might seem purposeless. If nothing else, the names of fallen kin are now engraved in this paper memorial that will be referenced in the decades to come, maybe outliving those who are now in grief. All of this brings comfort to the keepers of the memories.

Now for the rest of us, having pored over the contents of this book, we must accept a responsibility for what is newly entrusted to our own memories. This might require an imaginative leap in a world that now expects images to be as ephemeral as the spoken word, where experiences are shared and forgotten in the time it takes to click the heart symbol on whichever screen comes to hand. In contrast with much of our experience in the 21st century, marks made on the paper of this book will last for a long time, and it's appropriate that the corollary marks made on us by this paper should stay with us for more than a moment. We did not know the names listed here, but we're all participants in the social process that led to their deaths, and if you're reading this in later years, you can be sure that similar processes are at play. Someone somewhere is going to die for reasons over which we have no control but which are in some part motivated by the fact that we exist, albeit as atoms in society that is collectively a force.

We can hope that we are a force for good, but a force we are, and people will continue to die for our right to exist. Whether we consider ourselves passive observers or civic activists, pacifists or conflict hawks, patriots or renegades, Americans or global citizens, we are all participants in a larger process. We owe it not only to the unknown fallen but to ourselves to accept these memories for which we should be thankful that we did not suffer, and to understand something of significance from their remote losses. Even as these lives that are now past touch us from the pages of a book that they could not have imagined, some little action that each of us takes will have an impact on someone somewhere, maybe unknown and perhaps not even born yet. But be assured that even something as seemingly insignificant as the tiny objects photographed by Inbal Abergil can have consequence. From the desolate waste of personal loss she has created a message for us that speaks honestly and clearly about real-world events, and also encourages hope and optimism in those of us left to continue.

# ACKNOWLEDGMENTS

I wish to express my unmitigated love and appreciation for my husband, Tamir Harosh. I am deeply grateful to him for his love and belief, which always kept me going. For our children: Ohad and Ohri, who, enriching our lives, constantly remind us of what matters and inspire us to keep being better.

To my mother, Fabian Abergil, for her love, generosity, and encouragement. For always believing in me and making me believe that anything is possible, no matter what. You will always be my muse.

I have been fortunate to have my brother, Moti Abergil, whose long-standing support I am so grateful for. Thank you, Michal, Daniel, and Roy, for keeping us all together.

I am deeply indebted to the authors who contributed texts to this book—Fred Ritchin, Carol Becker, Stephen Mayes, and Maurice Emerson Decaul—for their invaluable words. Each of them has addressed my work in a unique way, amplifying our understanding of both its context and its content.

I want to thank Fred for his intellectual involvement during this project development and execution—his careful reading of the book and the time he spent with me on it.

I owe a continuing debt of gratitude to Sharon and Howard Socol, who shared my enthusiasm and kept a watchful eye. Their continued support and love for me and my family mean more to me than they could ever know. I want to express my gratitude to Lauren and Mitchell Presser, for their understanding of the importance of this project and for their generous support and friendship. I am grateful to Cathy M. Kaplan—her contributions were many, and I am grateful for them all.

The comradeship of colleagues and friends has always been essential to my vision of *N.O.K.* In that spirit, I offer my heartfelt thanks to Moyra Davey and Allen Frame, for their wisdom and insight throughout the whole process of producing this project and book. Their constant support and challenges I have enjoyed.

I am indebted to the constantly reliable assistance of Jackie Battenfield, who is always there to provide good advice. I extend special thanks to Sue Jaye Johnson for our productive brainstorming sessions in the beginning of this project and her encouragement. I offer my sincere thanks to Brian Turner and Col. Jack H. Jacobs for their important advice and inspiration. I want to thank my wonderful assistant and friend Jody Wissner, for her collaborative spirit and keen thoughts. Nelli Sheffer, my longtime mentor and friend, has been generous in his support of my vision from the beginning. My interest in photography and perception continues to be stimulated by conversations with Thomas Roma. I have also learned much from my colleagues at Pace University, Columbia University, and International Center of Photography (ICP), as well as from my students, too many to name, who have always made me work harder.

*N.O.K.* received support from Fiscal Sponsorship with Artspire, a program of the New York Foundation for the Arts; and also from the Visual Arts & Literature Office of Cultural Affairs, Consulate General of Israel. I want to thank Vick Giasov and Aviad Ivri for their warmth and support. Fujifilm has been extraordinarily generous with materials. Brandon Remler deserves special thanks for his continued support and understanding of the importance of this project. I am grateful to Baxter St. at the Camera Club of New York, which has exhibited and supported *N.O.K.* Many thanks to Michi Jigarjian, Libby Pratt, Susan Fulwiler, Saul Robbins, Izabela Jurcewicz, Pacifico Silano, Alessandro Teoldi, and Jesse Cesario.

The following friends and colleagues have helped me with this project in various ways, and I am grateful: Miguel Amado, Maya Benton, Elisabeth Biondi, Phillip Block, Elinor Carucci, Vincent Cianni, Insiya Dhatt, Mark Dion, Dan Duane and Deborah Lerner Duane, Lia Gangitano, Kirby Gookin, Janice Guy, Harvest Henderson, Tina Kukielski, Brian Laguardia, Jack Menasche, Rafi Musher, Ami Neiberger-Miller, Suzanne Nicholas, Claudio Nolasco, Jaime Permuth, Christopher Philips, Ethan Pierce, Yvette Raby, Anna and Giancarlo Roma, Leo Rubinfien, Elisabeth Sherman, Dana Sherwood, Ella Shohat, Matthew Sosnow, Kara Walker, Lilly Wei, and Alice Zimet. From A+L Center: Laura Gonzalez and Alexander Harrington. From Artis: Yael Reinharz and Rivka Saker.

I'm thrilled to have my first book published by Daylight. Special thanks to Michael Itkoff, who showed an immediate appreciation for this project and has helped make this project into a real book in the world. I want to thank Ursula Damm for her sensitive editing, sequencing, standing support, and elegant design. Copy editor Elissa Rabellino made many helpful suggestions.

Above all, my warm love goes to the Gold Star families, without whose help this project would not have been possible—families who had faith in what I was doing and who opened their hearts and homes for me. For continuous encouragement and inspiration, Emily Toro, a Gold Star mother, and Vicki Miano, a Gold Star sister, deserve special thanks. My deepest appreciation goes to Raul Lopez, who has given so much of his time helping, guiding, and teaching me so much about the Gold Star families. I am grateful for the care and concern you all have shown for my work. This is for you and for all the Gold Star families out there.

Inbal Abergil
New York, 2017